LATE LOVE

· ·

"So many Boomer marriages are ending in divorce that people are calling it the 'Grey Divorce Revolution.' Why? Men past 60 are stuck in the old patriarchal mode, and their newly empowered wives are having none of it. Whether you want to leave a long marriage or transform it, this is an inspiring read for an entire generation."

Terry Real, Author of The New Rules of Marriage, US

"Entertaining and educational, personal and practical, Late Love is more than its title suggests – those who love at any age can learn from it."

Marie C. Wilson, Honorary Founder and President Emerita, Ms. Foundation for Women
Founder and President Emerita, The White House Project, US

"A fascinating thesis on the need to reframe our approach to relationships - and expect more of them and of ourselves."

Robert Baker, Senior Partner, Mercer and Co-President PWN Global, UK

"I love the slogan "Grow or go!" This book will help many women shake off bad marriages."

Dr. Tessa Szyszkowitz, UK correspondent, Cicero.de, UK

"For all those who have made peace with loveless lives... there's still hope. And this book shows you why and how."

Anuradha Das Mathur, Founding Dean – Vedica, INDIA

"This book is both poetic and practical - and useful for both those in long term relationships and those in new ones. It's confronting for both, but is a reminder of the constant need to rethink, redefine and renew. I immediately gave it to my husband to read."

Margie Seale, former CEO, Random House, AUSTRALIA

"An aspirational clarion call to all those who yearn for fulfilling, stretching, mutually supportive relationships. Don't settle for anything less! Here is a roadmap for moving from mediocre to mastery."

Samantha Collins, CEO, Aspire, UK

"I wish *Late Love* had been available 20 years ago. Buoyant and charming, the narrative, examples, and research cited in this book attest to Avivah Wittenberg-Cox's personal experience of late love and professional documentation of late love's possibilities. Readers discover what late love looks like, why it is no intriguing, and how it can happen–for you, for me, for anyone who longs for a partner who is present, authentic, and willing to grow."

Mary R. Bast, PhD, Enneagram Coach & Mentor, US

"More and more people in the modern world are finding themselves - often unexpectedly - single in later life. The task that lies ahead of them is not only to come to terms with the loss of what they had imagined to be a commitment that would last until death. They also need to create for themselves a new future where the place of partnership is rethought. Avivah Wittenberg-Cox's book tells her personal story of *Late Love* in a way that offers insight not only to others in the same situation but to anyone mindful of the challenges that such relationships bring. Thoughtful, thought-provoking and a significant new addition to the self-help canon."

Susan Quilliam, Author, How to Choose a Partner, UK

"A beautifully written, deeply insightful and generous book. Written from the heart, it is a treasure trove of stories, invaluable tools, hints and tips for anyone evaluating their love life. Whether you are contemplating leaving, have left, or wonder what or who next – this book will be your guide and friend, helping you shape your thinking, gain clarity and ultimately take steps towards your own late love life."

Yasmin El-Dabi, Executive Coach, UK

"Sheer inspiration from a master of the possible. AWC's newest book gives us all a shot of much-needed reality-based positivism. Love IS POSSIBLE, no matter what your age or situation. Baby boomers: With courage and an open heart, your best days can be in front of you she shows us, with her own story as well as so many others. I smiled all the time I read it... except when I cried. Poignant, positive, inspiring. A must read for every generation. In other words, "go for it!!"

Davia B. Temin, President and CEO, Temin & Co., US

"At last a book for women over 50 who still want… everything! Totally logical that the high priestess of gender balance, Avivah Wittenberg-Cox, writes the book that so clearly reflects the current zeitgeist. This book rings like a warning alarm: the expectations of women – of themselves, of their companies and of their couples isn't lessening with age. It's only gathering speed. Be prepared to work to a higher standard, driven by late vitality, curiosity and knowledge. This should be mandatory reading for companies or spouses who say "I didn't know" when women walk out the door for better. With her usual intelligence, humour and courage, Avivah paints the portrait of our generation. Inspiring!"

Isabella Lenarduzzi, CEO JUMP Forum, BELGIUM

"Forget about 'adequate' marriages. *In Late Love: Mating in Maturity*, Avivah Wittenberg-Cox makes the compelling argument that later life love is not only possible, but that it can be filled with deep connection and passion. Part memoir, part roadmap, Wittenberg-Cox inspires you to re-evaluate all your assumptions about romance. You may even find a new one in the process."

Abby Ellin, journalist and author, US

"A blushing, unabashed, yet eminently sensible ode to new love in mid-life. Read it if you're serious about finding passion in your empty-nest years. Or if you're stuck in a dead-end relationship and hoping for the courage to leave. But especially read it if you're already half-way out the door and need someone to hold your hand as you leap into the unknown."

Stephen Snyder, M.D., sex and relationship therapist and author,
Love Worth Making: How to Have Ridiculously Great Sex in a Long-Lasting Relationship, US

LATE LOVE

Mating in Maturity

Avivah Wittenberg-Cox

Published by Motivational Press, Inc.
1777 Aurora Road
Melbourne, Florida, 32935
www.MotivationalPress.com

Manufactured in the United States of America.

ISBN: 978-1-62865-456-1

Contents

For Tiamo

"I wrote the story myself. It's about a girl who lost her reputation and never missed it."

Mae West

"A case for love as a skill to be honed the way artists apprentice themselves to the work on the way to mastery, demanding of its practitioner both knowledge and effort."

Erich Fromm, *The Art of Loving*

Love: Late
Avivah Wittenberg-Cox

The shock of sight
Surprised at sunset
Emerged from the baggage
Of early and before

Powerful light
Blessed our becoming
Relaxing at beyond
Thawing into being

Surprised by right
Wrinkled awake
Smiling from the swing set
Blinking back joy.

ACKNOWLEDGEMENTS

. . . .

Tʜɪѕ ʙᴏᴏᴋ ᴡᴀѕ ᴍᴀɴʏ years in the making, and would never have been published without the encouragement of many people along the way, some of whom appeared magically at just the moment they were most needed. Their enthusiasm for the book and its purpose gave me courage. I needed every ounce of it, as this more personal voice is far out of my comfort zone.

Who would have thought that I would meet a book publisher on a weekend sailboat excursion with friends in Sydney Harbor? Margie Seale was my first believer. I delight in such happenstance meetings with strangers which can be, if you are open to them, signposts to the future. Paul Saltzmann and Annie Peace for a glimpse of just how good late love can get, and their affirmation of the book's attempt to reflect it. My new best friend, Yasmin El-Dabi, was my first 'target market' reader. Watching her benefit from the book's ideas convinced me it could be useful to others. Susan Quilliam, one of the UK's leading relationship experts, who gave so generously and responsively of her time and welcome advice. Barbara Howson for her publisher's perspective on contracts, book covers and the reality behind many book publishing myths. Mary Bast is a wonderful coach and all-round wise women who's eagle eye and powerful heart has so often guided me through. I promised her I would, albeit sadly, never use an ellipse again … Nancy Lee and Marie Wilson read a draft aloud to each other with delight and then graciously line edited the hell out of it. Robert Baker gracefully agreed to apply a 'masculine lens' to the whole. And to all the writers, thinkers and philosophers I have learned from and so enjoy following, reading and retweeting: Alain de Botton, Stephanie Coontz, Sharon Jones, Eli Finkel, Alexandra Solomon, Esther Perel, Terrence Real, Helen Fisher, Pepper Shwartz.

I want to thank the dozens of couples across several countries and generations who generously shared their late love stories. Their happiness, youthful energy and capacity for re-invention inspired me. Role models, all!

To my children, who, though they didn't opt for the plot, were fundamental building blocks of its happy ending. I am forever grateful to their growing hearts.

To my mom, who taught me what love is.

And, of course, to my own love Tim, without whom the story wouldn't have been worth the telling.

PROLOGUE - THREE POTS OF JAM

• •

THE CULTURAL ANTHROPOLOGIST Margaret Mead once wrote that every woman needed three men in her life. One as first young love. One to be the father of your children. And finally, one to be your soulmate in full maturity. Who would ever have guessed that someone I had never met could trace my romantic life and loves so well? Since each of mine was particularly sweet, I've always recast this as my three pots of jam…

I have found that many people are experiencing the same trajectory. Life is long, and lengthening. Each phase of life demands that we grow and change. Our relationships need to be able to do the same. Some couples are able to negotiate these evolutions together, others will not. It takes two to tango, and unless both partners are willing to shift to a waltz, finding different dancing partners for different parts of life is likely to become increasingly common. A relationship that was a perfect, passionate introduction to love may not be the best match for having and raising children. And the father of your children may not be the kindred spirit with whom you dream of spending the thirty or more years now on offer after the children move on.

My first love, romantically enough, was a Frenchman. He was exactly what that word mythically means. He was utterly charming. And kind, and creative. He was the older brother of a friend I met after moving to Paris. He was seven years older than I was (as is my third pot of jam), and the eldest of three fun-loving siblings of '*bonne famille*,' a term that covers bourgeois families with well-brought-up children. He was everything a first love should be: a good dancer, a passionate sailor, a tender lover. And very tall. As a rather feisty short person, I have a serious weakness for tall men who make me feel small and protected. We dated for a couple of years, but I sped off to Brussels for a job, and he was, at 30, more interested in settling down – he was, in the end, too local to appreciate my international habits, and didn't speak English. He did, I am flattered to note, end up marrying a Canadian woman (I hail from Toronto with a French mother). Looking back, I must admit he was the very loveliest way to start. I was madly in love, not just with him, but with his family, his country, his language. Delightfully, in one of those lovely loops of life, his brother recently gave my son a job.

Next came the father of my children, and a loving and peaceful 22 years. We met in Brussels, but he was a boy from Buffalo, an hour's crow fly from my hometown. He loved Europe passionately, and has devoted his entire career to working towards its construction. We shared a lot of things: our North American origins, good educations, cheery and pragmatic outlooks on life, and international career interests that meant we could settle in the Paris he had always adored, with the French passport I contributed to our couple. It was a reasoned choice, a good match, and he was and is, through and through, a good man. He would, I'm sure I sensed, be a devoted husband and father. And he was. We had a very collegial and contented partnership. In our years together, we raised two adorable children, invested in work we cared about, and lived in harmony in a lovely old French house covered in vines. He did not, however, share my increasing concern that we might replicate what his parents had become: an uncommunicative couple who had grown apart over the years. As I aged, I yearned for more and more depth in relationships, and he did not. I like to think our parting was about as amicable as it could be.

My third man, and I trust my last, bears a strange resemblance, in many ways, to my first love. He is about the same height, also has a big, somewhat aquiline nose set between blue eyes, and an inexplicable passion for boats. He has the same sort of creative energy too, and multiplicity of talents. The same inability to focus too long on any one thing. The same incredibly charming way with women, who are most of his best friends. He has one of those delightful British accents that all North Americans find so attractive and intellectual. Backed up by a stimulating brain and love of all things aesthetic, intellectual and mechanical. A polymath, he is sculptor, sailor, lobbyist, and perhaps spy for all I know. And he is kindness itself. Kindness, I know, is probably the principal characteristic of my three pots of jam. Energy is next. They were each exactly right for each particular phase. I have not had relationships with many men, but have been blessed with relationships with the right men. I am deeply grateful to all of them, and for the arc and grace they have given to my life.

While society accepts, without a whimper, the shift from the first to the second pot of jam, the shift from second to third was dramatic, traumatic and hard. Did it have to be? Should we not be able to make contracts that are renewable, maybe every 20 years, to adapt to lives that will soon pass the 100-year mark? I'm as strong a believer as anyone in commitment and parenting and responsibility. Let's raise our children well. And then there are two. And time to re-evaluate, recommit, perhaps redesign. At work, we are accepting the idea of lifelong learning, new careers and transformation. It's time to accept it at home as well.

'Grow or go' will become the norm. It already is.

INTRODUCTION

· ·

JULIET, TALENTED AND successful as both businesswoman and mother, found herself bored and listless in a companionable but passionless marriage. Eventually, feeling if she didn't act she would lose herself and any sense of self-worth, she left her marriage of 30 years at the age of 55 and plunged into the unknown. Many of her friends simply didn't understand it. She has yet to find a lasting new relationship; yet the joy and sheer excitement of the last few years shines in her eyes. Turning 60, she looks forward to a future of discovery and self-discovery.

Andrea had experienced years of emotional bullying and belittling from her husband that left her depressed and deeply unhappy. This was clear to her friends, and even her children. Yet when she finally took the plunge and left her husband of 24 years, and her financially secure marriage, she found herself the recipient of criticism and condemnation by many, including one of her children. Happily, within three years she found new self-confidence, new hope and, above all, a new and deeply appreciative love that has transformed her life in a way that is transparent to everyone who loves her and has completely convinced those who had previously criticized her for what she did.

I had a picture-perfect marriage that, after 22 years, left me lonely and unsatisfied. After years of trying to get my husband to join me in defining a new dance, I waltzed out the door instead. And fell into the arms of a very old friend. We discovered what the term 'soulmates' really means. And I was astonished to discover that the profound happiness I tapped into radiated out beyond myself.

Why weren't these transitions easier, more encouraged, more celebrated? Late love seemed to me to be the cherry on the cake of life. Deep, wise and profoundly nourishing. I started to ask around, and found that others too were surprised by joy at an age when they had resigned themselves to love in the past tense.

In fact, it turns out there is an explosion of "grey" divorce and remarriage in the over-50s these days. It is driven mainly by women, and a minority of men, who are deciding that "adequate" marriages are inadequate. With children departing into their own journeys, and ever-longer lives stretching out ahead, more mature adults are leaping, unconventionally and aspirationally, at a last chance at love.

A majority of the existing literature discourages them. The dominant mantra of books, counsellors and media is that "staying together" is the superior, admirable choice. They insist that romantic dreams of great sex and soul mates are the Disney-esque yearnings of the naively immature.

I will argue the contrary. Great relationships are not only attainable; they are a natural and admirable goal for aging humans. And if your current mate isn't interested in working with you to craft an ever-deeper and finer partnership, then it may be your mate who requires changing – not your dreams.

For the past two decades, I have criss-crossed the globe as a writer and consultant on gender issues in business. I had always been interested in how issues of gender at work affected issues of gender at home. But when I decided that term limits were needed on my own long marriage, and discovered that late love had given me a new lease on the second half of my own life, the interest morphed into passion. I became convinced that many of the skills and self-awareness that made good leaders at work, also made good partners in life. So I began to ask friends a lot of questions. What was the promise and potential of consciously redefined relationships between partners at home in the second half of life? Did new gender roles contribute to new happiness? And especially, could we become masterful at love?

Late Love explores how today's explosion of marriages in the second half of life may offer innovative role models for mastering newly balanced relationships between men and women. The extraordinary changes in women's roles and the evolving needs of men are transforming today's couples. The results are perhaps seen most clearly in the surge of late unions being carefully designed and created today by men and women who are redefining gender lines at home, with the advantages of self-awareness, maturity and higher degrees of relationship skills.

Fulfilling relationships are a fundamental goal for a life well lived. The increase in marriages between people over 50 suggests it's never too late. But can it actually get better? And how? Can divorce be reframed as a creative claim to selfhood? Can our societies' aging lovebirds be role models and inspiration for love in a more gender-balanced world?

The book is a rich resource for anyone looking to find and build a mature, joyful union in adulthood. It's also a clarion call for all those who might like to, but are stuck on the fence, in unsatisfactory relationships, or recovering after the loss of a mate (through death or other, more hurtful, departures). Equal parts roadmap and inspiration, the book offers a joyfully fresh perspective on the naturalness of emotional transitions in lengthening lives. It charts a course for the journey towards late love: how to see existing relationships through a fresh lens, how to digest the lessons from the first half of life and how to make wise choices for the rest of the road.

This trend towards second-time-round marriage must be viewed in the context of an unprecedented, millennial shift in gender relations. As women's educational, social and economic empowerment increases, they continue to demand more for the world, and from it. This is true at home and at work. Settling for anything less than mutually supportive, seductive and stretching relationships is so yesterday. As the number of late leavers and lovers swells, their thirst for more is redefining what relationships look like in a greying, gender-balanced world.

And it looks pretty good.

I use my own personal experience and philosophical musings as a launching pad, and add interviews with couples who have consciously created and designed love in late unions. Divorce rates and marriage rates are both dropping overall, but the greatest increase in both is in the over-50s. Why?

My hypothesis is that we can achieve mastery in intimate relationships through self-awareness, hard work and intention, what Eric Fromm called the "art" of loving. The current view of modern marriage is that love and romance have conquered economics as the founding principle of the institution (described in Stephanie Coontz's *Marriage: A History*). But can the recipe of late love be grounded in the success literature (it's hard work and 10,000 hours of practice) and in the happiness literature (all humans are happier after 50)—so late love becomes the cherry on the cake for humans who focus on relationships as a prime imperative of later life? The research includes a wide sweep over the current global statistics on marriage and re-marriage in the developed world, debunking a few myths along the way.

The rise of women in the course of the twentieth century is pushing almost everyone everywhere in the direction of yearning for deep, satisfying and mutually beneficial – and above all more equal - personal relationships. Though, let's be honest, it's mostly women who are doing the pushing. Their growing social power, political influence and financial independence are redefining the rules of every game in town.

But, above all, love.

Love has come a long way in the last several decades, although I agree with the writer and observer Alain de Botton that we are probably only part-way through a long journey of learning how to master relationships. But I disagree with his constant (and beautifully argued) case that our ideals of romantic love are misguided and set us all up to fail at "good enough" relationships.[1] In my experience the only

---

1   Alain de Botton, *The Course of Love,* Penguin 2015. See also his blogs on love at TheSchoolofLife.com

people who hate the word 'soulmate' are those who have never found one. "We want a soulmate," writes the comedian Aziz Ansari, "And we are willing to look very far, for a very long time, to find one … but we want more than love. We want a lifelong wingman/wingwoman who completes us and can handle the truth."[2] Once you find them, you get why everyone is trying so hard. Because it's worth it. And, as the famous ad from L'Oreal used to say, because I'm worth it.

Of course, it didn't start with love. It started with freedom. When the contraceptive pill went on the market in the U.S. for the first time in 1960, it was an immediate game-changer. Within five years, as Jonathan Eig describes in his book, *The Birth of the Pill*, the age of marriage and childbirth had both increased significantly. Once women had finally captured control of their bodies, they could start negotiating the terms of their relationship contracts. Up until then, women were a means to an end (property, capital, progeny and cheap or free labour). Some countries are still trying to keep them there.

Suddenly, almost overnight, women decided they could be, not a means to an end, but an end in themselves. They could start working at better paying jobs, and fan out into ever-widening swathes of the economy and society. Today, just a short half century later, women under the age of 30 out-earn men in every major city in the U.S.[3] This is likely to be a precursor of what is to come in other countries, as women's education levels continue to outpace that of men. This shift has huge and often underestimated consequences at multiple levels – political, economic and social. It is at the core of a revolution in the balance of power in relationships.

This book looks at individual lives and stories, including my own, to tease out common threads and lessons. In each story, all the above forces can be seen at play, as in a microcosm. A record number of women are leaving marriages because, for the first time, they can. A massive wave of financially independent women is changing the data—and the institution of marriage—forever.

---

2 Aziz Ansari and Eric Klinenberg, *Modern Romance: An Investigation,* Penguin, 2015
3 Hanna Rosin, *The End of Men: And the Rise of Women,* Viking, 2013

Women are marrying later, having children later, having fewer of them (or none at all). They are leaving unsatisfying marriages more readily. In countries unfriendly to these changes (such as Japan or South Korea) women are presented with a choice *between* careers and family rather than policies to conciliate them. Where 30 years ago the result was a choice in favour of marriage and family, today many more are choosing careers, leaving large numbers of men unable to find the traditional wife they were brought up to expect. In these countries, national birth rates are falling through the floor, leading to aging populations and shrinking workforces.

It's a dystopian view of the future if we get the shifting gender rules wrong. Countries, companies or couples not supporting the new roles and aspirations of both men and women may find they end up with *The Economist*'s redefinition of the weaker sex: men.[4]

Yet, as many of the stories in this book also show, if we can embrace the changes, and enable both men and women to explore new roles and skills, we may create some of the happiest and most gender-balanced relationships the world has ever seen. Not to mention healthier and more equitable societies and economies.

Sprinkled throughout the book are a series of personal essays written in a more intimate voice. I have been writing these for a long time, to help me think through life, but have never published them. Big choices in life entail a dialogue between head and heart, and in most people one of these organs has a distinct dominance. I've been raised and educated in a rational world, as you may have noted from this introduction and any of my other books. I have been taught to convince with facts and data and argument. The real me, though, at this stage of my life, is all about heart. I've unleashed her, in my life, and in these pages. Just a bit, in boxes…

---

4   "The Weaker Sex" (cover story), *The Economist,* May 30, 2015
     http://www.economist.com/news/leaders/21652323-blue-collar-men-rich-countries-are-trouble-they-must-learn-adapt-weaker-sex

HOW THIS BOOK IS STRUCTURED

This book is rather different from previous books I have written and, I freely admit, is a bit of a 'wanderfest' across the categories of self-help, sociology, autobiography and creative writing. It mixes together personal experience, interviews, societal trend data, analysis, personal musings, poetry, practical toolkits and resources and, towards the end, some short personal essays I wrote along the road of this extraordinary journey into late love and which express in a more metaphoric form many of the emotions I experienced.

The first section, **Leaving**, is about assessing whether a relationship has run its course. This covers a range from the truly toxic to the merely mediocre marriage. In increasingly long, ever-evolving adulthoods, our human longing for connection will eventually judge "adequate" relationships as totally inadequate. When the gap between expectation and reality becomes untenably large, it's time to walk. We will look at how to walk well, or how to compose with being left. Both involve grief and the loss of an idea and a dream.

Looking is about the self-knowledge necessary to unlock mature love. The strength to be alone, to think, to understand the patterns of previous relationships. If self-love is the key to loving someone else, how do you design the time and space to look before you leap anew? Do you know what you want and why? So often, people I interviewed found the human they ended up loving was often entirely different than the person they thought they were looking for. This chapter also visits the bizarre world of dating - including the new world of online dating - after decades of marital devotion.

Loving explores how consciously and intentionally successful late loves design their unions. Late love can benefit enormously from our earlier experiences, allowing us to strive actively for 'mastery' of love, particularly for couples who didn't achieve it first time round. The intensely loving relationships I delighted in discovering were based on full awareness and acceptance of three different pieces of the puzzle: oneself, the other and the relationship itself – a kind of secret garden continually weeded, nourished and cared for by both partners, in a way that combines the instinctive and the designed. It looks at shifting gender roles and expectations in later life, and the consequences for issues like power and money; the new patterns and rituals that can be established to avoid old mistakes and welcome new and more creative expression; and the lifelong learning about oneself and others that happy older couples radiate out around them.

Contentedly re-coupled, my final section looks at **Leaping**. Where do you go from happiness? The purpose of loving at any age or stage in life, and why we search for it so ardently, is to maximise the growth potential of both partners – and of their union. Marriage in life's latter half has different objectives than in the first 50 years of existence. It's not to have children and build a career, an identity and a reputation. It's more to find partnership in maturity, someone who loves the *you* you have become, and to support the dreams of the latter half of life. For some, it is consolidation and celebration of accomplishments. For others, it's new risks, new adventures and new personas. At its best, late love becomes a springboard for leaping; we stand with our partner on the highest diving board, look over the edge and joyfully leap, hand in hand. I leap and he holds me; he leaps and I hold him. We plunge and swim across the unknown waters of life's late life lake, towards shores we will dream, together.

Daring Again
Tim Hollins

As we let go, together,
   strange things happen;
Our senses expand,
New and urgent voices
   insist, entwine and bind,
Forbidden questions prick
   and pierce the sterile air,
Calling 'reality' to account,
While unexpected truths
   draw us on, demanding trust.
And, high above the clouds and fog,
   falling, we fly.

Then, gazing in each other's eyes,
New worlds and endless horizons
Dance on pupils; and the eye-spark in each
Heralds a new sun, chorus-calling,
Dawn breaking warmly on this proud land,
Reflecting back, in mirror-black,
The distant shore, discovered,
Close, familiar and touchable,
If only we dare again to plunge.

LEAVING

Choosing to Choose

*"In longing, we move and are moving from a known but abstracted
elsewhere, to a beautiful, about to be reached,
someone, something or somewhere we want to call our own."*

David Whyte

MEDIOCRE MARRIAGES

• •

For years, I couldn't admit it, even to myself. For someone who is seen by almost everyone as a self-confident and fairly strong woman, denial isn't my daily bread. Nor was vulnerability.

The whole world thought we had the perfect marriage. Even my husband had convinced himself of the fact. Who was I to disagree? To say that the lovely kids and home, the secure salaries, the thriving careers were not enough. To dig below the surface and see that all the subtle dissatisfactions of a long, conflict-avoiding marriage could accumulate into a massive disconnect with my spouse. And worse, with myself.

My mother was shocked.

Shocked not only by the news, but perhaps even more by her own non-knowing. I'm close to my mother. I must have been putting on a pretty good act.

At the beginning, the act was for myself. It probably started around 40. A bit of boredom with the repetitive routines and absent-minded relationships of the typical over-dedicated parent of our kids-come-first generation.

All was fine for years. We were well matched and mutually supportive for a good long time.

Dissatisfaction grew as the children grew. The bigger they got, the more impatient I became. My husband was a wonderful father of small children, just as his parents were before him. In fact, my husband was the archetypal family man. He loved his family beyond anything, and devoted his life and his energies to them. The family came before everything, including his couple, or himself.

While this worked well when the children were small and time-consuming, it worked less well when they were teens demanding freedom. I've long thought that children are a lot like cats and dogs. Very much puppies when young, they throw themselves on your heart and soul with an ardency unmatched by any other love. It is heady indeed to be the most important person in the world for someone. For some, it becomes addictive. Being needed and necessary becomes a huge part of their identity and offers many the primary meaning of their lives.

But as children move into teenage-hood, they turn into cats. Independent, temperamental beings who only deign to sit on your lap at the time and place of their choosing. And they turn on their magical purr only if you know exactly how and where to stroke… Dogs love to be needed, and will celebrate your arrival home with all the exuberance of a three year old. Cats accept only independence, and allow you to feed and pet them only if you've understood and obeyed their rules.

The essential role of parenting has always seemed to me to enable children to grow from dog to cat. And to leave, happily and capably, to carve out their own lives, with a flick of a mildly superior tail. But this independence cuts both ways. In *The Art of Loving*, Erik Fromm writes that a mother's key role in life is to be happy. In this way, she offers children the psychological belief that optimism and happiness are possible. This resonates with me, and I have accepted that my happiness is a duty to my kids and very particularly to my daughter. The ultimate feminist position. To care for oneself in the belief that will empower one's offspring.

As parenting has become an increasingly high stakes, high investment game, parents are over-investing in their children their own ambitions, identities and time. This has not helped marriage.

Parents are often simply too tired, too stretched and too wrapped up in their kids to spend the kind of time a mature and evolving relationship requires over decades.

A wonderful life coach I have worked with, Mary Bast, once sent me an outline of four phases of marriage.

1. **Love, projection, "you're just like me."** This is the phase where you feel you have met your perfect match, and revel in all your similarities.

2. **Work, commitment, children.** The middle part of marriage is about building many things: identities, families and/or careers.

3. **Crisis, "you're not like me," disappointment.** At some point, most relationships hit a reality that disappoints. You're partner is not what you thought. They don't live up to some idea you had of them. You feel dismayed, perhaps even betrayed.

4. **Work it through and realign.** How couples work through these kinds of crises is key to successful long relationships. Both need to be willing to lean in and work it through, for the benefit of both. This takes intention and attention.

Long-term marriages take work. They require work on oneself, and they require working together on the couple you create. Couples can be very much more than the sum of two individuals, but it helps if the individuals have done their own work on themselves. It takes two to be married.

So I worked hard. I worked hard on myself, and I worked hard at the couple. Looking back now, I feel a little sorry for my younger self. A bit embarrassed at my optimism that I could sort marriage out, just like I had sorted out so many other things. Just by focusing, and choosing and talking. Despite quite a lot of heavy hitting, I clearly failed.

I became a certified executive coach in 2000 and in the process learned a lot about myself. I spent several years as a visiting coach at INSEAD, a global business school based in France, listening to hundreds of business students just starting out in life. And I spent subsequent years coaching hundreds of executives in a variety of companies and countries. In 2007, unimpressed with my own marriage and my attempts at renegotiating it, I signed up for a year-long leadership program with the institute where I had done my coaching training.[5] It involved four week-long sessions in Spain, over the course of a year, figuring out one's own style and its impact on others. I decided to go with a twin goal: to figure out my style, relative to others, and its impact on my husband. It turned out not to be a particularly comforting picture.

After assorted physical, emotional and psychological contortions in a gorgeous old stone manor house overlooking the Mediterranean, I had a sunlit view of the patterns my husband and I routinely circled through. I could draw them on a piece of paper: my need for autonomy triggering his insecurities which made him redouble his efforts to pull the family together, which triggered my feeling claustrophobic, which triggered his fears of my leaving, which made him increasingly defensive, which made me feel more unseen and unheard. And round and round we'd go. Every couple has their patterns. Until they become visible to both parties, relations between two aging individuals fall deeper and deeper into their reactive, well-trodden ruts.

It is intensely depressing. Especially if one of you begins to see the patterns so clearly you can draw them on a page, and know what happens next with your eyes closed. And the other doesn't. Or doesn't want to. Because then your heart closes, too. The more I learned and listened, the more I saw the patterns. And the more I saw them, the less I wanted to keep repeating them.

One of the exercises in the leadership program was to inch along with a partner on two parallel tightropes, 30 feet off the ground. The only thing keeping you upright was a pole you held between you. The trick was for each partner to lean back just enough, holding their end of the pole, to allow

---

5   CTI, The Coaches' Training Institute

the other person to stay upright. As you inched along sideways towards your goal, this balance was constantly being renegotiated, without words, just with a sensitivity to the pressure being asked for or suggested through the pole. It was a brilliant exercise, and none could have been a more graphic metaphor of marriage.

It takes two people in constantly renegotiated balance to maneuver along the tightrope of life. And balance requires second-by-second adjustments to another human's moods and needs. If you stop adjusting, you fall off the tightrope. Period.

My partner for this exercise was a very religious fellow. He kept invoking Allah throughout the program. On the tightrope he was leaning way back, pulling on the pole. For a while, I hung on for dear life, asking him, increasingly desperately, to lean in, lean in, or he would pull me right off my precarious perch. He didn't, and my arms pretty soon gave in, aching at the strain of trying to lean against someone who weighed twice what I did. As soon as I fell off, so did he, of course, having lost my limited counterweight.

The funny thing was that as soon as he fell off, he came over to reproach me for not having had enough confidence in him. I hadn't trusted him. He was absolutely convinced that he had been doing everything in his power to keep us afloat. He was very disappointed in me. The group looked on in stunned disbelief, as it had been visually obvious what had happened up above their heads. It wasn't until he saw the video footage of our efforts the next day that he was able to see that he might have had some responsibility in our fall. Up to that moment, it had all been my fault.

Turns out, it was also a perfect metaphor of my marriage. If you stop adjusting, you fall off. My ex-husband and I weren't able to *lean into* our relationship to address the emotional issues percolating under the surface. Figuring out and renegotiating your respective needs is a complex and necessary marital moment at mid-life. It is particularly difficult if you have not learned this give and take early on. It is never too late to learn to dance together – but the key criteria is for both people to be willing to learn some new steps. One person leaning in while the other leans out or doesn't pay attention is asking for a fall.

How many million couples live in this kind of asymmetry?

I find we were not alone. Many men are, like my husband, good men, doing the best they can in the ways they know how. They have been raised to be breadwinners and consider that their major duty. Many modern men have taken a far more engaged role in fatherhood and are deeply connected to their kids, often at their wife's urging. So, many say, as did a young, male MBA student I told my story to, how ungrateful could I be? What do I expect of men then? What more can I ask of a husband than to be a good father, a loyal spouse and a sharing roommate?

The quick answer? Love. I expect, want, crave and need love. Including physical love. Erica Jong wrote in a *New York Times* that "physical pleasure binds two people together and lets them endure the inevitable pains and losses of being human. When sex becomes boring, something deeper is usually the problem — resentment or envy or lack of honesty." And that is true of marriage as a whole. When one partner wants out, or is bored, something deeper is usually going on. While women seem curious and ready to scratch and dig and discuss what that something might be, men still seem dauntingly uncomfortable with such discussions. Yet unless each partner can be fully honest, both with themselves and with each other, long-term partnerships are doomed to a sort of "roommate syndrome," where two people live together in friendly indifference.

Nina is a successful entrepreneur who lives on the other side of the world, in New Delhi, India. Yet her story and her desires unexpectedly echo mine. She had a picture-perfect marriage that lasted 16 years. But then she felt, in a subtle and almost imperceptible way, that her marriage was blocking her becoming the person she was able to grow into being. "My husband always felt I was a bit 'too much'," she explains. "Too generous, too kind. He was indulgent, he could accept the way I was, but underneath, he expected that I would come around, calm down with age and time. But on the contrary, I was hiding or under-playing the stuff that I was actually most proud of. I gave money, helped people. He felt I needed to be protected from the world. He came from a place of entitlement, I came from a place of gratitude. He thought the world would take advantage of me. I wanted to be more me than the person I was becoming for him…" She woke up one day and realised that "by making my husband's life perfect, I have sacrificed mine."

On the other side of the world, Lucy discovered the same thing after she found that her husband of 28 years was gay and having affairs on the side. Married at 22, sexless for 15 years, she just went along, figuring that it was a good marriage "in every other dimension." "I didn't realise how much of myself I had given up for my marriage. We did his stuff and I went along. I didn't even realise that we didn't do my stuff. I'd rather go to a Rolling Stones concert than the symphony, but we never did. When I moved out, I had to figure out what my own hobbies and interests were. Who am I? I had fused into him, and let him lead."

Poets tap into this sentiment best, and into its non-communicative harshness. "Silence is frightening," writes David Whyte, "an intimation of the end, the graveyard of fixed identities. Real silence puts any present understanding to shame; orphans us from certainty; leads us beyond the well-known and accepted reality and confronts us with the unknown and previously unacceptable conversation about to break in upon our lives."[6]

---

6   David Whyte, *Consolations: The Solace, Nourishment and Underlying Meaning of Everyday Words,* Many Rivers Press, 2015

After Love
Sara Teasdale

There is no magic any more,
We meet as other people do,
You work no miracle for me
Nor I for you.
You were the wind and I the sea—
There is no splendor any more,
I have grown listless as the pool
Beside the shore. But though the pool is safe from storm
And from the tide has found surcease,
It grows more bitter than the sea,
For all its peace.

There are a million marriage books suggesting ways of staying together, like the famous John Gottman book, *The Seven Principles for Making Marriage Work*. He says he can predict early on, in 15 minutes of a video interview, based on elaborate mathematical equations, which marriages will last and which won't. He identifies the distinct behaviors that he calls the Four Horsemen of the Apocalypse. When they appear, he can predict that they will, sooner or later, rip people apart:

1. **Criticism** – the kind of meaningfully laden comment that packs a much bigger punch.

2. **Contempt** – when your partner makes you feel small or worthless or wrong, often with just a word or glance.

3. **Defensiveness** – taking on the victim role, making your partner feel like they are the one who is overly demanding difficult or downright weird.

4. **Stonewalling** – an avoidance strategy, like leaving in the middle of a discussion so that you can never have the conversation that is needed.

Usually the first two lead to the third and then one partner (more often the male in his telling) retreats behind the fourth. For me, there seems to be another issue I think is most destructive of all, both gentler and more damning. Indifference.

"Everything that is essential is invisible to the eye."
Antoine de St-Exupery, *The Little Prince*

What really killed my marriage was that I simply no longer cared. There was no feeling. It died one day, flipped off like a light switch after a few years of fruitless efforts to reconnect. Like many women I know at midlife, I felt I was entering my very best years. For the first time in my life, I was happy with myself, beyond proud of my kids, engaged with my work and passionate about what I was doing in the world. A late bloomer, I had finally become who I was meant to be. And while the world, and my friends, and my soul were applauding and supporting and egging me on, I had the feeling that my husband was uninterested, threatened and hiding his lack of support behind a veritable wall of seeming support and perfect fatherhood.

This first smacked me in the face the day I finished writing my first book. I had always wanted to write. Both my parents were academics. Books and writing have been my closest, most intimate companions for much of my life. Inexplicably, I never really thought I could, or would. I flirted with some journalism early on, but I didn't know any writers or publishers, and my initial education had made me a computer coder, not a writer. Confidence, at the time, was not my strength. And moving to France had separated me from my writing language for decades.

I finally mustered the courage to step into writing through work. By 45, I had become a somewhat recognized player in gender issues. With the help of a friend, I pitched a book at a publisher, and then recruited another friend to help me edit the result. I was 47 years old when I pushed the send button on the final manuscript. My co-author, Alison Maitland, and I sang and hugged and hooted our way (via Skype) about our respective houses. The kids, when they came home from school, were appropriately impressed (and probably relieved). My husband arrived home late, and we sat directly down to dinner. He asked me how my day was, and I told him, with barely concealed excitement, that the book was done and sent in. He raised his glass, clinked it with mine, said, "Congratulations," and turned to my daughter and said: "And how was your day?"

I was totally, utterly taken aback. Speechless. How had we come to this? The complete denial of what is most meaningful to another person. Or not even knowing what is meaningful to them anymore. Or not wanting to know … or not agreeing. It probably wasn't intentional, it may not even have been conscious. I wondered if I had done something similar with his dreams and desires. I felt suddenly I did not recognize the relationship. This wasn't what I thought we had built. I was left standing on one side of a deep precipice of separateness. It was profoundly lonely. Lonelier than being alone. You are finally expressing who you are, what you believe in, and there is something about that expression that is uninteresting or even off-putting to the man you share your life with. It was profoundly dispiriting.

There was a second seminal moment that marked me, at the opposite end of the emotional spectrum. We had taken a short weekend in Italy, in a little B&B overlooking Lake Garda, in one of those attempts at relationship repair. Next to us at breakfast, sitting at a small table in the idyllic Italian garden, was a couple, lost deep in conversation. The woman was obviously very upset, and she let a veritable deluge of words pour forth. The man was leaning in, listening intently. Suddenly, she burst into tears and buried her head in her hands. What he did next had an unexpected impact on me. As I watched him quietly pull his chair around and lovingly – and wordlessly – hold her close, I burst into tears of my own. In that gesture, there was deep love, understanding and maturity. He wasn't trying to fix anything. Just to comfort, and be there. That, I thought, is what I want. The ability to be weak, and to be vulnerable. To cry and melt and be met – with both comfort and the permission to be utterly undone.

It was the sum of these two stories that captures what I (and so many strong, successful women I interviewed) are aching for. They dream of being admired for their talents, and empathized with for their weaknesses. They want to be encouraged to be as strong as they can be. And they want to be small and weak on occasion. The full range of being human.

Sadly, I think many professional women still get typecast at one end of this spectrum. They are a bit too strong, even over-powering. We don't fit the gender stereotype. We get labeled as "bossy," as Sheryl Sandberg[7] was, or told by our employers that we are a bit 'too ambitious.' At home, everyone gets used to us carrying things, organizing everyone, and caring for everyone's needs, emotional and otherwise. So we get stuck in a caring role, and lose the option of being cared for ourselves.

---

7   Sheryl Sandberg, *Lean In*. Knopf, 2013.

Our strength eliminates our option to be vulnerable. And we lose out at either end. Our strength threatens, and our weakness isn't recognized.

Martin Seligman, the father of positive psychology, in his book *Flourish*, defines three criteria for the condition we call a good life:

- Happiness (love and connection)
- Engagement (using your strengths and skills at mastery)
- Meaning (contributing to the world and a wider community)

As I was coming close to my 50th birthday, I realized I had the last two, but not the first. And I think that is where too many bright, successful professional women find themselves. Skilled, engaged and contributing to the world but not fully loved or known at home.

How many million women find themselves in similar circumstances? Eager to journey deeper into the second half of life with a long-time partner, to explore together the shifting phases and challenges of aging and maturing, and to discuss how to renegotiate and realign a relationship to nourish two human beings to become fully … human? Why is it that women relish this sort of thing and so many men find it difficult? I know they often like it when they actually do it, as I have seen hundreds of men exploring these issues at work, through the intense leadership development and coaching interventions that have now become the mainstream reality of senior executives in any large organization. But why are they more easily convinced to engage by their work than by their wives?

At this later stage of life, many marriages are largely amicable—and dead. Two people that habit and financial interests have bound together in comfort and boredom. Where the effort of pulling it apart just seems like too much work for uncertain returns and where the dull but known togetherness of marriage is deemed preferable to the unknown loneliness of solitude and encroaching age.

I felt I was simply drowning in the annihilation of self that came from pretending all was lovely when in truth it was not. It wasn't what we said or did. We were impeccably civil. It was simply what we had become.

And, I discovered, I was far from alone.

FROM "FEAR OF FIFTY" TO "FINALLY FIFTY!"

During most of my adult life and marriage, I had almost no close friends who had divorced. Our social circle looked like it was made up of fairly contented couples. Until I started getting within spitting distance of fifty, and suddenly everything changed. In the space of one year, half a dozen of my closest girlfriends walked out the door of long-term marriages. I was amazed. Some of them I knew and accompanied on the journey out, others had slowly matured their escape in the privacy of their own thoughts. All acted suddenly and decisively but all were acting on a long (in most cases painfully long) and thought-through decision.

I read Erica Jong's autobiography, *Fear of Fifty*, in preparation for writing this book. She is a very short generation older than I, 20 years, but I found her feelings and fears at midlife a very great distance from mine, or my friends. We are separated by more than age, of course. Although we are both Jewish, she is American born and bred and I am a mish mash of Canadian and European and chose to live my adult life mostly in France. Where she delayed child-bearing until very late and fully explored her generation's ground-breaking sexual liberation, I had a far more conventional debut. Married at the average age of 27, after a totally unadventurous start with men, I had my first child at 30 and my second by 33. And stayed solidly and securely married to the same man for 22 years.

Before I married, I had a degree in computer science and comparative literature, had moved to Paris and gotten a job with L'Oréal as a computer programmer. Later, I added an MBA. More importantly, I had an internal conviction that the world was my oyster. By the time I came along, companies and business schools were mostly looking for women, not discriminating against them, and I profited from the shift. I'm sure it helped me get into business school, and enjoy France, with its reputation as one of the world's most female-friendly countries (more on that later).

Mothers are key to the discussion of selfhood—and marriage. Erica Jong spends a lot of time in her book (and in therapy) understanding the impact of her mother's life on her own ambitions and fears. Her mother was forced to give up her career as an artist because of the pressures of motherhood. The result was that her daughter avoided motherhood until late, determined not to get similarly trapped.

I had a very different role model at home. My French mother loved my Swiss-German father, and after the two of them were tossed about the worst of Europe's mid-20th century carnage and Holocaust, they emigrated to freezing cold, Catholic Quebec in the 1950s and then on to Toronto. My father was a brilliant young math professor destined to do great things. But he didn't live to see his intellect deliver on its promise, was felled at 36 by a brain tumor, leaving my mother, who didn't speak a word of English, to fend for herself in a strange city with three children under 8.

She did. She went back to school for the first time since war had interrupted her studies in her young teens, earned a Masters in French language and literature, and became a professor herself. She was a wonderful mother, strong and smart and warm and loving. Intensely committed to her children, and very engaged in her work. What is the impact on me? Almost the opposite of Erica Jong … that women can do anything, that combining work and family is the norm, and that being amazingly strong and beautifully feminine is a natural combination.

In my long career in gender and women's issues, I have often found that many of the early powerful women come from women-led households. Single mothers prove to any girl early on that hard work and sheer lack of choices make anything possible. Mothers who work also remove from their daughters the insidious guilt implanted in the kids of full-time moms, that they are not giving their children "as much" as their own mothers had given them.

Mothers also have a huge impact on men. My friend Marian insists the only men worth loving are those who have good relationships with their mothers. I agree. Also with Margaret Mead's vision of the three key men in a woman's life: the man you first fall in love with, the man you have children and raise a family with, and then the soulmate with whom you finish your years. Some people are lucky enough to have some of these rolled into a single person. But I suspect for many, as for me, this segmentation holds true.

It would have helped if others had held this natural evolution of relationships up as a model. My mother lost her beloved husband too young, and envied my stable couple. She often repeated that in our family, we don't divorce. Thinking, then saying (blurting it rather one New Year's Eve to a friend as my resolution) that I wanted to leave my husband, then actually doing it, were the hardest things I have ever done in my life. I have wondered since why it should be so hard, and why we can't find a less traumatic way to bring relationships to an end. Recently moved to London, I discovered with delight that the School of Life, created by Alain de Botton, offers a series of workshops called A Good Separation. Brilliant and necessary, I wish I had had access to this a few years back.

So let me conclude on mothers and motherhood. And throw another rock in the pond. In the end, I also left my marriage for my daughter. She was only 14 at the time. I wondered whether I should wait, like so many do, until my youngest had flown the nest. In the end, and after much mulling, I decided this would be part of my own motherhood legacy. I wanted to give her a more flexible role model than the world offers us now. I wanted to teach her that if you don't love, you leave. And that you can leave lovingly. When leaving, I would stay close, even when my kids or my friends spurned my advances, and stay, and stay, and stay, until each individual heart had had the years and moons to heal, and move on. Mostly, I wanted to show my kids what "alive" looked like. I did. Now, I hope they too will settle for nothing less. Even if it takes a lifetime.

"Nothing has a stronger influence psychologically on their environment and especially on their children than the unlived life of the parent."

C.G. Jung

LEAVING TO COME HOME

"These boots are made for walking," I thought as I saw the pair of shiny black boots in the shoe store at Barcelona airport. I bought them. It took a few more years until I finally mustered the courage to walk out of my marriage. As it happens, I actually drove away. Music blaring, Lara Fabian's Urgent Desir on the radio calling for a blank page. "Tout effacer, recommencer." I wanted more and less. So I drove off, in my little red Mini packed with the bare minimum: a salad bowl and the painting of the big, red pregnant woman embracing her promising curves.

Blazing down the driveway, gravel squealing, I drove onto the street, breathless and exhilarated. I didn't even feel like turning for a last look at the beautiful old home I had found and loved and raised both children in. I wanted out. Unencumbered by the empty shell my beloved home had imperceptibly become, crack upon inexorable crack. A lovely picture of a common lie.

Things are so often not what they appear, a lesson each life delivers sooner or later. My son, my soulmate, had just left for college. His sister's panicked phone call left him un-shelled, his snail soul abruptly retracting from the trampling of his treasured, happy life. His childhood ended not when he left home, but when home left him. He abruptly learned to mistrust his own ability to read reality. He hadn't seen the truth behind what he wanted to be true. Most don't, until they can't do otherwise. The loss of innocence is shocking, as gale-force winds hit the haven some manage to construct within their own four walls. The seeming perfection was no protection in the end. Untruths never are. The reality behind many a mask ranges from the mundane to the monstrous. I can claim only something in between: the creeping malaise of indifference. The drudgery of pretend, the unapologetically unsaid, the deadening earnestness of avoidance.

A Monday morning after New Year's, after returning to work, I took a lesson from a colleague about time management. "Start with what matters most," she had advised a younger me. So after toasting my daughter's bread just so, and buttering it lavishly, I watched my girl (a rear-view-image of my younger self) make her way down the drive, shoulders already starting to sag under the growing adolescent weight of all she was not. I settled into the deep, grey blue softness of our living room sofa, determined to start the year I'd turn 50 by taking control of the rest of the road. It was time. For me, for her. I wanted her to learn that so many of the world's maps were not designed by —or for—women. It was up to us to draw our own. I carefully composed an email escape. And so began the long journey home.

Three years later, I was packing up again. My daughter has just graduated from high school in Paris, my son from college in LA. I was moving to another country, and so were they. As we began to spread out around the globe, appearances again deceived. It looked like we were moving further

apart, and yet I had never felt closer to either of them. A friend, watching my son and I chatting on a hotel couch during graduation commented, "It is so obvious that when you are together, you are both home." The walls of this home have been a lifetime in the making. They are as invisible as they are indestructible, built in the rock of mutual love. Only the rare, astute gaze can discern their true power. Within this haven, there is not a room without the possibility of laughter. Truth, in all its forms—from harmony to hardship—blows through unannounced. There is no dust that settles. And love licks at our heels whenever we walk out the door.

My daughter is just starting her journey. She has hated these last few years—and, like too many girls—herself. She is tiny in stature, with a long, thick lioness's mane of hair. She still asks me to butter her breakfast toast. She knows I will put on all the butter she now refuses herself. And everything else besides. She is off to Switzerland this fall for college. We will drive down together in my little red Mini. And I will hand over the keys. They will, I hope, help her leave home—and find it.

WHY WE STAY AND WHY WE GO

It takes years. Literally. No one walks out the door on a whim. It took me more than five. Reading just about every book about love and divorce along the way. This didn't help much. The overwhelming message of most of the relationship literature is leaning toward having you stay and work things out. Couples' therapy is the same.

Everyone seems to couch staying together as some form of success, and breaking up as some form of failure. This is particularly true of marriage therapists and counsellors, to whom couples in trouble go for help.

Alain de Botton has summarised this view in a New York Times article that stayed on the best-seller list for months, titled *Why You Will Marry the Wrong Person*. He says the dream you have of a mutually loving and supportive partnership is idealised naiveté. It's a Hollywood myth, stuff you have been sold by soap operas. In the real world, the only person you can change is yourself. Satisfy your own needs by developing friends and networks and work you believe in. Don't project your dissatisfaction with life on your partner. Accept your partner's imperfections, and recognise your own. Become mindful, Zen and healthy. Appreciate all you have, and develop gratitude. Grow up. Get over yourself.

This works, for a while. But if only one partner is dancing, you'll quickly find your new moves are leading you to shimmy, ever more skilfully, directly to the exit. If both of you are ready to learn to dance, it can lead to either a new bridge or a widening gulf between two people. To work, both partners must be willing to play at self-discovery. And it's a million times more effective if you begin the discovery before you hit the bumps in your relationships. If only one partner works hard at self-knowledge, and the other won't engage, won't self-question and/ or denigrates the other's efforts, the gulf simply widens.

The gender divide on these questions looms large. Women seem, on the whole, to love this stuff, and are always the majority of coaches, therapists and psychology students. Katherine Woodward

Thomas, the author of *Conscious Uncoupling* is a typical example, a self-admitted "change junkie, ever pushing the edge of my own and others' evolution in pursuit of fulfilling the potential we hold." Her ex-husband, like so many of the men I interviewed, was more positioned in the space of "total acceptance and appreciation of things as they are, without the need to change anyone or anything."[8] It is usually women dragging men to couples' therapy. Men come to it far more reluctantly.

The growing group of masculinity experts, like Michael Kimmel[9] , point to a culture that shuts men down early. They are raised to be strong, silent and rational, "like a tree," jokes Kimmel. Parents still tell too many young boys not to cry. The equivalence of masculinity with a rejection of emotionality shuts down half the population's emotional intelligence. It doesn't help their partners either. Couples expert Terrence Real points to our overriding patriarchal culture that holds everything feminine in contempt. He routinely sides with women to get their husbands to actually listen – and hear – what they are trying to say.

Working on oneself at least has the benefit of clarifying one half of the equation. I highly recommend it. Learning to know yourself, your impact, your needs is an essential part of becoming human. You can spend quite a number of years "working on yourself." I certainly did. I became a certified coach a decade before I left, and accompanied hundreds of people through their work and life choices. I became adept at a vast range of tools routinely used in the corporate world to support individuals in understanding themselves, their colleagues and their environments: 360 interview feedback (where you get feedback about yourself from direct reports, peers and bosses), personality tests of all kinds, and a year-long leadership program. I also threw in yoga, meditation and some mindfulness. Whatever works. I felt pretty good about almost everything in my life.

This contentment threw into ever-greater relief the piece that wasn't working. You can throw yourself into work, and achievement, or you can calm yourself down with breathing through your

---

8   Katherine Woodward Thomas, *Conscious Uncoupling: The 5 Steps to Living Happily Even After,* Houdder & Stoughton, 2015
9   Michael Kimmel, *Angry White Men: American Masculinity at the End of an Era,* Nation Books, 2013

downward dogs, but if the problem is an issue you need to thrash through with a partner unwilling to meet you halfway, you're simply going to return to the point where many of us start: will you stay with something some part of you is screaming isn't right? Or will you toss yourself into the unpredictably stormy seas of the unknown to see if you can find better?

Many people in this phase have an enormous fear of the potential loneliness of being on their own. A friend of mine is reduced to a complete panic at the idea of returning to an empty home, no matter how unsatisfactory the other inhabitant might be. Yet this dread often underestimates the degree of loneliness one can feel with a mismatched partner. I found it deeply, profoundly lonely to be with someone I no longer loved. "Longing is the transfiguration of aloneness," writes the poet David Whyte. "Like a comet's passing tail, glimpsed only for a moment but making us willing to give up our perfect house, our paid-for home and our accumulated belongings…" Being alone beckoned as a peaceful harbor.

Another friend, Andrea, stayed years longer than she now thinks she should have. She was staying, like so many of us, "for the kids." Three teenage children proved a persuasive glue to her abusive husband, who subjected her to routine humiliations, weekly budgets and a general withering of her own self-esteem to near-suicidal levels. She eventually left one sudden spring weekend, pushed to breaking point and in survival mode, before any of her children had left for college (the classic breaking point for a majority of fragile unions). In retrospect, she's glad she did. She now sees that the key question is, "What are you role modelling for your children?" Her two daughters and son had become used to seeing their mother reduced to tears by an uncaring husband flexing his psychological muscles. Today, they are proud of the mother who left and redesigned her life on her own terms. They are close and supportive. Her eldest daughter read a toast at her second wedding that brought tears to everyone's eyes, acknowledging her dash for happiness as inspirational and empowering. Tellingly, both daughters are now more interested in marriage, something they had earlier sworn they would never fall for, dismayed by the model in front of their eyes.

Although I love the idea of lifelong partnerships, I only love them when they are happy and mutually nourishing. There are very few of these around. I could look around my social network and count on one hand the couples I think of as anything I would hope to emulate. More often I wince at the undertones of tension or disrespect that glare out of so many relationships. As one journalist wrote, that "garden-variety mental cruelty you probably saw traces of at your last dinner party."[10]

I was most struck by a cousin of mine whom I was congratulating for a 30-year anniversary. I wondered aloud how people made it that long. He replied, "Lack of courage." That was one of those light bulb moments for me. I swore I would never say the same thing.

THE LEAVERS AND THE LEFT

It is important to admit that this chapter on leaving is entirely written from the point of view of a Leaver, someone who chose to leave their marriage, not someone who has been left. They are two entirely different species. They are at different places in their lives and in their heads. The Leaver is in control and plants the bomb that disrupts the existing order. The Left is in the uncomfortable situation of having to cope with a decision over which they often have no say.

It is astonishing the degree to which the Left have narrated the story line. Since Virgil's *Aeneid*, Dido's plaint has been followed by a veritable deluge of mourning by those left behind. We understand so well the pain of being abandoned, for having heard it so often, in poems and films and novels.

"So, you traitor, you really believed you'd keep this a secret, this great outrage? Steal away in silence from my shores? Can nothing hold you back? Not our love? Not the pledge once sealed with our right hands?"

Aeneid, Book IV

---

10   http://www.telegraph.co.uk/men/relationships/10357829/Why-do-women-initiate-divorce-more-than-men.html

The storyline has been swallowed and internalised. That the Leaver is a cruel, insensitive person abandoning home and family in a selfish and largely illegal dash out the door. Some of my friends assumed this to be true, or took it as their own story. This adds to the agony. You question your feelings, no matter how insistent, casting yourself as selfish and self-centred. You second-guess your sense of reality, weighing the harm you will cause and downplaying your own pain. Then you find some unexpected friends and family who judge you exactly as the person you never wanted to be: cruel and insensitive. Every interviewee who had been a Leaver said they lost people along their transition no matter how justified it was.

This is partly inherited from an earlier time, when it was the perception that most Leavers were men in their 50s abandoning their non-working spouses to find fresher fare. They left too many women and children as the economic shipwrecks of their midlife transitions. But the scene, and the story, have shifted. Nowadays it is mostly women who initiate the journey out the door.

According to the U.S. National Center for Health Statistics, women are the ones who file for divorce in two-thirds of cases—and this for as long as there have been records. When the couple is college-educated, divorces initiated by the wife climb to an astonishing 90 percent. "For the past 100 years, the primary filer has been the woman. The divorce rate began climbing at a drastic rate in the 70s. This statistic correlates with the fact that beginning in 1969, U.S. states began adopting 'no fault' divorce laws and by 1985, all states had such a law in place."[11] (The UK still has no no-fault, immediate divorces.)

Most divorces (66 percent in the UK, about the same in the U.S.) are caused by women walking out. The reasons for this are widely interpreted. For some, it's that men are somehow more willing to put up with sub-par marriages, while women are still optimistic enough to strive for something better. That the vast majority of men quickly remarry, while the majority of women do not, suggests men

---

11   http://www.yourtango.com/experts/cindy-holbrook/top-10-reasons-why-women-divorce

have more trouble surviving without a spouse. Women's networks of intimate girlfriends offer support and friendship, while so many married men let their wives manage the social side of life.

But while the reality of divorce has shifted, and a far more economically empowered generation of women is now gaining control of their destinies, the story around divorce has been left hostage to the sad sentiments of the Left. The tale of mature, thoughtful women carefully negotiating an exit from an unfulfilling or abusive relationship is far less common. As is the depiction of joy and freedom they feel as they put their feet on the pedal of their futures.

The Leavers are embarrassed, saddened and guilty. They have caused hurt and turbulence to people they love. Children who wanted nothing to change. Women aren't used to being selfish, or making a ruckus. It's the first time for many of them. But it's a story worth telling those still sitting on the fence. It will take years to decide, to work at staying, to accuse yourself of a lifetime of crimes. But in the end, there comes a time, perhaps only a moment, where you know. It's time to go. You embrace the pain, recognise it as part of adult life, and walk straight into – and through - it. It's awful, it's harder than most anything else you will ever do. There will be pain and panic and days of darkness. And it's the only way to claim your future.

Mary Oliver, an American poet, may have said it best, in a famous poem that was the mantra for my own journey:

The Journey
Mary Oliver

One day you finally knew
what you had to do, and began,
though the voices around you
kept shouting
their bad advice—
though the whole house
began to tremble
and you felt the old tug
at your ankles.
"Mend my life!"
each voice cried.
But you didn't stop.
You knew what you had to do,
though the wind pried
with its stiff fingers
at the very foundations—
though their melancholy
was terrible.

It was already late
enough, and a wild night,
and the road full of fallen
branches and stones.
But little by little,
as you left their voices behind,
the stars began to burn
through the sheets of clouds,
and there was a new voice
which you slowly
recognized as your own,
that kept you company
as you strode deeper and deeper
into the world,
determined to do
the only thing you could do—
determined to save
the only life you could save.

The interviews conducted in this book are with a combination of Leavers and Left. Many Leavers spoke of it being both the hardest decision they ever made, and the most empowering. Interestingly, the decision to take charge of the rest of your life seems to continue into finding a new partner. Most of the Leavers I interviewed took a highly proactive approach to finding another love. Grounded in the same energy that propelled them to lucidly think about their situations, try and work it out with their spouse, and then decide to move on and out the door. A mixture of courage, self-knowledge and the conviction that love exists, fuels the subsequent search for a future partner. They long for something they feel certain exists, a determined reaching out to claim a part of themselves – the loving, lovable human within.

THE TROUBLE WITH MARRIAGE COUNSELLING

One of the challenges for marriage counsellors is the gap between Leavers and Left. Usually the partner who wants out is the one who initiates some form of counselling, in an effort to see if somehow there is a way of "making things work." The success of these efforts is as rare as the statistics about their efficiency.

Terry Real, a leading American couples' specialist, summarizes the problem for many couples: "Women feel unheard, and men feel under-appreciated." Women, as the majority of Leavers, are usually asking for men to become more like women, says Real. To talk, share emotions and vulnerabilities, and perhaps above all, to be empathetic listeners who know to resist the temptation of offering prescriptive, fix-a-problem solutions. This is a tall order for many middle-aged men. Especially as the work world is usually asking them for the opposite: to be unemotional providers of quick solutions. The CEO of a global headhunting firm told me over lunch that he had just been on a weekend with three of his closest friends, all of whom had recently been left by their wives. They were, he said, completely shell-shocked, and had no idea why they had left. They were loyal, hard-working, and successful. Wasn't that enough?

The answer, in this age of liberation, is no. It's no longer enough. Many women in the latter half of life are financially independent—at least enough to scrape through on their own. The costs and burdens of child-rearing are behind them or on the way out. As time frees up for post-family women, their focus often returns to the couple. And they want more from it. A lot more.

The challenge is that many marriage counsellors put both partners on an even footing, and try to facilitate a mutually satisfying outcome. But they are often dealing with partners who are at dramatically different psychological and evolutionary phases. Leavers have typically spent years getting to the point where they managed to get their partners into counselling. The Left is often a reluctant and sceptical participant, undermining the process as much as possible. This dichotomy is beautifully depicted in the film *Hope Springs*, with Meryl Streep and Tommy Lee Jones. The classic older couple, she is hungry for romance and connection, while he is emotionally mute and uncomfortable—and convinced he is right.

Therapist William Doherty, has identified this gap. He understands that most couples counselling assumes that two people are coming to fix a relationship. He also recognises that this misdiagnosis inevitably leads to the failure of any kind of therapeutic intervention. Doherty estimates that for 30 percent of couples he sees, one partner is coming to counselling in order to leave, while the other is there in order to stay. He's developed an approach called 'discernment counselling' to help therapists with a triage at the start to figure out what is going on and adapt the response.[12] He proposes a 6-month period of work, with divorce off the table, where couples are invited to decide if the relationship is viable. At the end of this period, the couple can separate with both partners feeling they did what they could, and made a reasoned decision. His is still a rare voice.

The gender stereotypes around women's emotionality and menopausal disturbances don't help with any of this. Some men think their wives are just upset by menopause, and that they would "calm

---

12   William Doherty, *On Discernment Counselling,* http://onlinelibrary.wiley.com/doi/10.1111/jmft.12132/full

down" in time if they just hung on and ignored the fuss. Therapists do both parties a disservice when they don't recognize the reality of gender imbalances and emotional skills in couples.

Different therapists take different approaches. Some, like Doherty, try to see each partner separately, to gauge where they are individually before witnessing the patterns in action. A very few, like Real, take a clear position in recognizing that the majority of women (at least among the boomer generation) are emotionally more mature and expressive, and defend their demands to overly self-righteous and uncommunicative men.

But in the end, most admit that by the time it gets to a counselling situation, it's too late for the majority of couples. The Leaver is halfway out the door and the Left hasn't even begun to wake up.

It's not always clear-cut, of course. Lucy was both Leaver and Left. After 28 years of marriage, she discovered that the man she had married at 22 had decided he was gay and had been having a string of affairs for several years before she found him out. She had read a range of weak signals (including no sex for 15 years) but had let herself simply believe it was all good enough not to rock the boat. They had a friendly, companionable partnership, she had questions but sublimated them, and decided she could live with the situation. Until she learned the whole truth, and suddenly her entire life was up for reinterpretation. She could not live with the double life, and the other men, and the hidden bank accounts and credit cards. She was the one who ended up leaving him, and asking for a divorce. He would simply have liked to continue things as they were, in a gay revision of the old-fashioned mistress story. But in the eyes of her friends and family, she was seen as the Leaver, and lost a number of friends who judged her for breaking up the perfect marriage.

Lucy got a double hit. She received all the suffering of the Left, feeling abandoned by the man she thought she knew. And all the judgment of the Leaver, who is rebuked by people's assumptions, fears and projections.

AN ENTIRELY NEW DECADE ... OR TWO

One of the trends supporting the explosion of late divorce is the increased health and vitality of older adults. My mother thought she was old by 60 (although she is still crackling at 90). Now most of the 60-year-olds I know are vibrant, super-busy people keen on travel, new careers or new hobbies. One of my role models in life is an extremely elegant woman in her mid-seventies who still works full-time heading up the special reports section of a major current affairs journal.Barbara Beck, who heads up the Special Reports section of *The Economist* magazine. She is an extremely elegant 72. These new realities mean that when children go to college, there is still a long stretch of active living ahead for their moms, that keeps getting longer.

Just as 20-somethings have a relatively new and free decade in their 20s as ages of marriage and child-bearing have gotten increasingly later, so do 50-somethings. With children gone, and new attitudes to aging, encouraging people to be active well into their 70s and 80s, the pressure on marriages increases. As does the societal acceptance of older couples forming in later life, in a variety of married or co-habiting formats.

So new questions will increasingly arise:

- After 20-something years of marriage, do I want to spend another 40 years of my life with this person?
- If I want another jab at love, should I jump while I'm still relatively young and attractive ... and have at least a decade or two of health and vitality ahead?
- If my partner were to fall ill in the coming years, am I ready to lovingly support them?

These are two relatively new adult phases in human history: the 20s and the 50/60s. You used to be settled, married and a parent by 25. Now the average age of marriage for women is 30 in the UK, 28 in the US. So the 20s have become a time of exploration of adulthood, full of experimentation and travel and questions. Similarly, the decade after the departure of children used to mean retirement, health issues and grandparent duties. Now the older set is in a similar state of exploration, experimentation and questioning. What will they do in their Third Age? Will they continue to work, start a new business, move to philanthropic or artistic pursuits? The percentage of new companies started by older workers is exploding, too. Decades formerly seen as a time of decline are becoming an adventure in mature self-discovery. A new—and exciting development.

Unlike the 20s, the post-50-year-olds explore this phase with enhanced self-knowledge, experience and—often—a much greater degree of financial freedom. The big expenses of life are behind them. Kids and college are finally digested, many at this age have paid off their mortgages, so major costs are often in steep decline. And, while stories and stereotypes of poor aging women abound, the reality of the gender balance of assets in the future is less well known. Women in the US are set to inherit 70 percent of the money that gets passed down over the next two generations, in addition to what they already earn in income. They already own more than half of America's investable assets.[13] This offers a whole new freedom of decision-making.

Many women now in their 50s and 60s have earned significant incomes. This is the first massive wave of women financially independent from their husbands. The choice to stay or to go is ever more firmly based on the quality of the relationship, not on the liquidity of a bank account. It's a whole new game. And another pressure on marriage at this age and stage.

One of the realities of aging is that you are looking at decades where you are likely to spend an increasing amount of time alone with your spouse. As your children get busier with their own lives, as your own careers eventually gear down, or as health becomes a limiting factor on mobility, there comes a time where you know you are going to be spending a lot more one-on-one time with your partner.

That was the hard reality that hit me. Marriage had been a time of so much busyness. I had been over-brimming with people all around—kids and my own business, and colleagues and travel and

13   Boston College Center on Wealth and Philanthropy

friends. But as the children start to move on, one is suddenly left with a first taste of what is to come. Dinners are no longer noisy affairs where everyone is angling to get a word in edgeways. It becomes a resoundingly quiet dinner à *deux*. For healthy couples, this is a time of renewed energy and projects and conversation. For the rest, it is a sobering *hors d'oeuvres* to the rest of life— and endless dinners yet to come.

The other difference between the post-50 decades and the 20s is the question of mortality. In your 20s you feel you have an endless sweep of time stretching invisibly ahead of you. By your 50s, the horizon has dramatically shortened. The biological clock that once nudged you into having children now returns and nudges you into evaluating the use you have made of your life. You have inevitably started to witness the death of parents, friends or loved ones. You have no idea whether your own luck and health will hold. We all become gamblers in the crap shoot of life, but the odds of decline steadily increase with every passing year. So the pressure to use your time, wisely and well, to live life to the full, starts to build. Slowly at first, but with an insistent knocking at each new piece of bad news about someone you know.

My good friend Annabelle, single all her life, told me that if she died tomorrow, at age 67, her one regret would be that she had not experienced a committed, stable partnership. This is part of what is giving her the courage to try … before it's too late. She has been falling gently, carefully and somewhat fearfully in love over the past few months, with a man she met at their respective mothers' old age home. Her age, and the ticking of the clock, is strengthening her resolve to make it work, to swallow a powerful cocktail of pride and fear, and choose love.

Another friend, who was my age, fell ill with Lou Gehrig's disease just shy of her 50th birthday. For two years, I had a front-row seat watching her swift and heart-wrenching decline. It felt like a signal from the sky. Live the time you have consciously and appreciatively, because it can come to a shattering end at any moment.

For me, these various pressures distilled into a simple question: do I really want to spend another 20 years or more increasingly alone with my husband? Do I really want to spend the next year here? The answer had become so obvious I could only begin debating the timing of my decision.

So the wonderful gift of the extension of life by several healthy decades ends up putting marriages to a new test: the test of time. This wasn't as often true a generation or two ago. Many (especially men) died shortly after retirement – that's how the retirement age was designed.

We have been gifted with entirely new phases to adult human life, wonderfully outlined in *The 100-Year Life*.[14] We will have multiple phases of education and several different careers over the course of ever-lengthening lives. We will want to learn how to transition constructively through them and not be surprised by change at every turn of future unpredictability. So it is time to accept and acknowledge that many of us are also likely to be blessed with more than one long-term, committed partner. And we will need to learn how to create lasting, mutually enriching relationships, and how to leave them, lovingly and well. A skill that very few people have yet fully mastered.

LEAVING WELL

So what does it take to be a masterful Leaver?

Different people had very different takes on this topic. Some of the key ingredients of those who managed it best included three key steps: time, preparation and connection. Some of my interviewees did this particularly brilliantly. But most, like me, muddled through doing the best they could but feeling like they failed at some fundamentals. So think of this, if you go:

---

14 Lynda Gratton and Andrew Scott, *The 100-Year Life,* 2016.

1. TAKE YOUR TIME

The rule here is to be proactive but not reactive. In her book, *Dancing with Intimacy*, Harriet Lerner describes in detail what this means. In short, it's about getting to the point where you can communicate about difficult issues with those closest to you without becoming emotionally "hooked" into their issues, patterns and habitual reactions. This is no mean feat. It takes most of us years of self-reflection, maturation, and forgiveness to get there. It's about finally being absolutely honest about your feelings and your decisions, without being emotionally overwhelmed by the reaction.

I must admit, I copped out here. I had always found it difficult to talk about personal issues with my husband. So I had, through the last few years, gotten into the habit of trying to communicate with him through writing. For me, this was a way of carefully modulating my tone, and being as loving as I wanted to be, which I found impossible in face-to-face interactions. I worked on my final missive, the one where I announced my decision to leave, carefully and sent it to him just as he was about to get on a train for a long trip home. I thought it would give him time to react and digest a bit before I had to sit down with him. It did not go down well. I would not do this again. In retrospect, I still would have written it, but I would have handed it over while we were both at home.

Martha did it much better. She brought up the subject directly, took the time to address it with her husband over many months, then invited him to discuss it with a therapist present. He was convinced that she simply wasn't serious, despite all her explanations, until she physically walked out the door. His deep belief that she wouldn't have the courage to leave, and his conviction that they had a great life, blocked his willingness to hear what she was trying to express. But all her preparation had given him the choice to engage, or not. Her patience and pacing allowed this decision to emerge, slowly but surely, rooted in reflection rather than just initial reaction. By the time she left, he had made a clear choice not to try and address the underlying issues, and was then honest enough to let her go lovingly. They worked together to make the split as friendly and cooperative as possible.

2. PREPARE EVERYONE

It helps to make sure you give key family members time to digest the news before anything happens. Ideally, with the two of you sitting down with each individual and explaining why you are separating and what you are planning to do around a whole series of key issues that will be of prime concern to whom you are talking. This is, of course, especially true for children. Sitting down with children as a couple, and calmly explaining that this is a joint decision that they are not, in any way, responsible for. At perhaps no other time in your entire marriage is unity in communication more important. And while I realize this may be an impossible ideal for many couples who separate in strife, it is an absolutely key part of helping your loved ones through the inevitable turbulence. This is also true for parents, and other family members, as well as close friends.

A little explanation—and not too much—goes a long way. Like every other part of a healthy communication, carefully preparing a jointly agreed-upon message that is clear but not too detailed helps get through the hugely emotional minefield that can be unleashed by news of a breakup. For children, it is so essential for them to know that they are still loved and will be cared for by both their parents, and that their parents will continue to get along and act as mature adults, especially regarding their care.

Aileen did a great job of this. After a 30-year marriage with a passive-aggressive man she had met at 15, she finally decided to leave after a bad car accident left her incapacitated for a while. To her disappointment, she discovered that her husband was completely unable to support her while she recovered, remaining entirely dependent on her despite her condition. It took her two more years to digest this shock and get ready to leave. She began by telling her husband, then together they carefully sat down with their two children to explain what was going on. They gave them time to take it all in, and told them they wouldn't start the separation till they were ready. Eventually, she moved close by, so that the children could go back and forth at will. This gave everyone years to adjust and minimized the disruption to the children's lives.

I really did not take the above steps well at all. Because my entire marriage had been conflict-free, my children thought we were a happy couple, a welcome contrast to so many of their friends' horror stories. They were completely shell-shocked by my news, which was delivered when my son had just returned to college on the other side of the world, and so the two siblings who were so close had no one to turn to as I delivered my time bomb. Again, I shamefully admit that it takes so much courage to move, I grossly underestimated the preparation, timing of the news, and joint delivery of the message for the kids. I rushed when I should have paced.

Juliet decided after the fact that she had spent time trying to explain too much about her reasons for leaving to too many people in her social circle. She realised she had been trying to care for and manage other people's feelings, when in the end, she had little influence on the impact of her decision on others. A break up always triggers other people's stuff: the state of their own marriages, the scars of their parents' marriages, a vast myriad of religious or other beliefs you may or may not share with them … this is not in your ability to manage. Nor is it your responsibility.

You will inevitably lose some people along the way. I did. Some surprising friends and family, people I had known for decades, would not even discuss my decision with me. They just cut off communication - for good. Now, when witnessing friends' split-ups, I prefer to remain carefully neutral. Judging other people's relationships is pretty impossible. But I also learned that those you lose in transition probably weren't very good friends in the first place. These moments have the benefit of making those realities visible. You really do learn who your friends are, and that, I think, is one of the great gifts of divorce. As the philosopher Seneca wrote, "Those who have failed stand amid vast loneliness, their friends fleeing from the very crisis which is to test their worth.[15]"

These moments have the benefit of making those realities visible. You really do learn who your friends are. It is one of the great gifts of divorce.

---

15   Seneca, *Letters from a Stoic*. Penguin, 2015

3. STAY CONNECTED

A separation ends up being experienced very much as an abandonment of the Left by the Leaver. While the Leaver is usually excited and energized by their dash for the future, the Left is usually in pretty dire straits, as are the children. This is where pacing the exit, and staying closely connected in whatever ways you can, becomes essential.

I stayed in the house for six months before physically moving out to my own apartment. I just moved into a separate bedroom. A totally surreal state of affairs, but helpful I think in somewhat reducing this feeling of abandonment. For years, many Leavers stay closely connected with their upset exes, offering support and a receptive ear. For too many men, their wives are their closest human connection, and the only person with whom they can be completely open and vulnerable. Some don't have many close, intimate male friends, while most women usually have several. These men are hardest hit as they discover the inevitable escalation of events as their spouse moves out and they begin to discover life on their own. So finding an acceptable level of continued communication with your spouse is very helpful to keeping the situation as friendly and constructive as possible.

For children, it goes without saying, staying connected is key. This can be difficult, and every child will react very differently. One of my children (who was away at college) was fairly understanding—or at least tried very hard to be. The other was much, much angrier, and it took a couple of years to repair the relationship and rebuild trust. It also took daily proof that I was still there, still engaged, still a mother. There were many times where she wouldn't talk to me, wouldn't engage, and I lived through two years of sleepless nights worrying how to keep the connection alive.

Daily texts and lots of emails are a wonderful form of one-way communication with a recalcitrant teen. You can show you care, and keep caring, no matter whether they respond or not. It paid off in the end, and we are closer than ever. But it was certainly the very hardest part of the whole, and almost entirely unexpected. I never in a million years thought I'd have a problem with my kids. We were so close. That, of course, was the problem. Shows just how dumb and unprepared I was! So be forewarned, even children as close to you as can be may push you away for what can seem like an impossibly endless time. Prepare them as best - and as gently - as you can.

A NOTE ON THE ULTIMATE LEAVING

There is, of course, another way of leaving that I won't pretend to cover, but can't ignore either. That is the issue of dying. There are currently 13.6 million widows in the U.S., and almost a million more being added each year. The average age of widowhood is 59, says Kathleen Rehl, the author of *Moving Forward On Your Own*, a financial guide book for widows.[16] Rehl describes a wide range of issues for these widows, that share some, but not all the characteristics of the Left described above.

One of the issues is the gender imbalance among those left behind. Widows outnumber widowers four to one. Eighty percent of widowers remarry within three years, while for widows between the ages of 55 and 64, the number is 8 percent. For widows over 65, the number is 2 percent. Why the dramatically different numbers? Rehl laconically explains that widows, who often cared for their dying spouses for years, don't want to be, for this last life phase, anyone's "purse, nurse or mother." The other reason, nicely summarized by behavioral economist Dan Ariely, is that "women are their husband's best friends, where the reverse is not true."[17] Women have better social networks, he says, than most men do, so are more able to survive contentedly, surrounded by friends and family. The result is that "80 percent of American men die married, while 80 percent of women die single."[18]

However, in the UK, the data tell a different and more optimistic story. Increasing longevity means the number of both widows and widowers is dropping, The gap in life expectancy between men and

---

16   Kathleen Rehl, *Moving Forward On Your Own: A Financial Guidebook for Widows,* Rehl Financial Advisors, 2010
17   Daniel Ariely, speech, Chautauqua Institution, July 24th, 2015
18   Kathleen Rehl, speech, Chautauqua Institution Women's Club, July 2015

women is closing as healthier lifestyles allow men to catch up with women. This, combined with more progressive social norms, are allowing people to cohabit with partners later in life – outside of wedlock. The UK has only 205,000 widows over 70, down from over 212,000 a year earlier. And the number of elderly couples living together outside marriage has more than trebled over the past decade. So the number of women over 70 living alone for any reason – divorce, separation or widowhood – has fallen by 5 percent. In just a few years, the number of over-70s cohabiting has doubled to over 150,000.[19] People who lose spouses or leave them are increasingly finding themselves late loves. An encouraging testament to the powerful attractiveness of partnership in later life.

There are obviously great differences between being left by someone dying versus someone walking out the door. While the devastation may be comparable, the anger and resentment differ greatly. As one interviewee told me, "When your husband dies, you don't have to deal with him and his demands for decades. And neither do your kids." Divorce and separation are complicated by having to negotiate an entirely new relationship with a huge part of your social network, including your most intimate connections.

Widows often complain of losing some of the social capital that being part of a couple still brings in most cultures. But they are more likely to preserve some of the things divorce often leaves in its trail: especially financial capital. Over the next decade, it is said, women will control two thirds of consumer wealth in the United States and be the beneficiaries of the largest transference of wealth in the country's history. Estimates range from $12 to $40 trillion. Many boomer women will experience a double inheritance windfall, from both parents and husband.[20] Private bankers, take note!

---

19 *Telegraph,* http://www.telegraph.co.uk/news/health/elder/11726529/Britains-vanishing-widows-cohabitation-and-men-living-longer-transform-old-age.html
20 Claire Behar, Senior Partner and Director, Fleishman-Hillard

IN THE END ... LOVE OR FEAR?

The final choice about leaving in most of the interviews can be boiled down to something starkly simple: choosing between love or fear. Ask yourself if what is holding you in place is love—a real attachment and fondness for something or someone—or is it fear—of the unknown, your ability to cope, or the consequences? Then decide which of these two emotions do you want to devote the rest of your life to.

One of my interviewees described it well when she explained what finally made her move: "I didn't want to become a bitter woman, or someone I didn't respect. I saw it among my mother's friends, the resentment, the wasted lives. Rather than blaming themselves, they blame their husbands, or others. I could see myself heading down that road. I was getting less and less pleasure out of life. Things that used to make me happy, stopped."

I chose love. For me, it was the best decision I ever made. It was also the hardest. It takes courage and stamina and staying power. But it's worth it. Seven years on, I wish I could have known most of what I learned too late, and am trying to share in this book. But at the time, my heart was telling me, more and more insistently, what my head really didn't want to know. I was scared. Terrified. Of a million things. Yet you can only ignore the deadness for so long before you become a brittle and unpleasant version of the human you are able to become. And while the naysayers will shriek that you are being selfish and ignoring the needs of others, there is truth in the oxygen mask metaphor they tell you about on planes. You have to put your own mask on before those of your children. Only if you can breathe can you save others. And only if you love yourself can you be loved and love others. In the end, I went for love, and got it back, tenfold. The joy of being oneself, and loved for it, is the ultimate reward of a lovingly crafted exit.

• • • • • • • • • • • • • • • • • • • •

THE TOOLKIT

• • • • • • • • • • • • • • • • • • • •

Trying to decide? Here are some sources of inspiration that I found particularly useful.

WHEEL OF LIFE

This exercise invites you to take a step back. Look at your level of satisfaction with all the different dimensions of your life. Rate your satisfaction with each of the 8 areas of life on the circle, on a scale of 1 (low) to 10 (perfect). Draw a line across each pie section, so that you have some sort of an inner circle across all the dimensions. Is it a smooth, consistent wheel, or does your wheel have jagged edges? A smooth wheel is not necessarily what you are looking for, but the jagged edges hint at what you may choose to focus on.

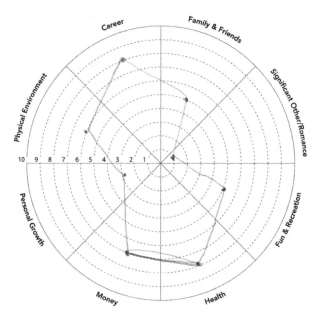

Are you highly satisfied with most of the other dimensions of your life, aside from your romantic relationship? If this is the only area that is much lower than the others, then you are right to focus in on this particular issue. But if several of the dimensions are low, you may choose to address some of the others first, as some of your dissatisfaction might be coming as much from them, as from your partner. Many people blame their partners for frustrations that come from entirely different parts of their lives. Being contented and satisfied starts with taking full responsibility for your life – your whole life.

LOVE OR FEAR?

To help clarify what is driving your choice, or your indecision, look at what is tempting you to leave and what is anchoring you to stay. What is it that you most appreciate about your current situation, and what is it that you fear? And if you were to leave, what are your dreams and what do you fear losing? Compare your lists, is one side of each answer much longer than the other? If your decision to stay or go is anchored in fear, ask yourself if that is the emotion you want to live by?

STAYING		LEAVING	
What I Love	What I Fear	What I Love	What I Fear

CHECK YOUR FEELINGS

We are very good at letting our heads get the better of our hearts. I find that deeper realities are usually screaming at us through our bodies and our energy levels. Energy is one of the great engine oils of happiness. Some people give you energy, other people leave you feeling depleted, and life is much more enriching with the former. The older you get, the more you want to start choosing the people you surround yourself with. Start by creating two lists:

1. The people who give you the most energy. Where you come away from conversations with your own energy boosted and positive feelings in your heart and/or head.

2. The people who seem to drain energy away. Where every interaction leaves you depleted and tired, and feeling a little less than the person you were just a moment before.

Where is your partner on these lists? Becoming more conscious of your real feelings often means simply recognising and accepting what you are already feeling. Denial and fear are powerful forces at shutting down your emotions.

Intentionally observe them, and write down what you see.

- Does your energy level rise or fall when your partner arrives or leaves?
- How do you feel waking next to your partner?
- What about when either of you goes off to work in the morning?
- How do you feel when you hear your partner's key in the front door lock?

The answer to many of the big questions are in the tiny, repetitive moments of your every day. If the answer to the above is you feel like the energy is draining from your very bones, it may be time to acknowledge it.

WHO SUPPORTS YOU?

We all need support to get through life. We don't need to get all of it from a single person. However, it is shocking for some to discover just how little support they get from their own partners. Write down in the left column the names of the people closest to you in the world. Then put a tick to indicate what kind of support

NAME	Emotional	Physical	Intellectual	Spiritual	Logistical

you get from each one. Are you well supported in each area by someone? Are there any particular holes that may require addressing, or people who don't support you in any way at all? How is your partner positioned? Many of the people in this book decided or discovered they simply weren't supported at all by their own spouse, or not in crucial times of need, and that shocked them into realising that they really deserved better.

What have you concluded from these exercises? Are there any patterns emerging?

BOOKS

I read a library of divorce and relationship books. Here's my short list. Not too many, just the seminal works:

Terrence Real, *How Can I Get Through to You? Closing the Intimacy Gap Between Men and Women,* **Simon and Schuster, 2003**

Terrence Real is one of the leading couples' therapists in the US. His major distinguishing feature is the muscular approach he takes to acknowledging the power differences between genders in most couples. He is very ready to confront men with what he calls "patriarchal contempt" for what women are asking for: to engage emotionally. He's a broad, conceptual thinker, and gives a lot of useful tools for analysing and presenting graphically what's going on in relationships.

Pamela Haag, *Marriage Confidential: Love in the Post-Romantic Age of Workhorse Wives, Royal Children, Undersexed Spouses and Rebel Couples who are Rewriting the Rules,* **HarperCollins, 2011**

Haag takes a deep dive look at the low-conflict, low-stress unhappy marriages that she calls a "post-romantic," 21st century phenomenon. She writes that "in the gloaming of the romantic age, we've valorized marital mediocrity, and called it realism; we've vilified marital ambition and called it selfish. Consequently, at a time when marriage could be anything, we very often expect it to be less." The majority of these seemingly stable marriages lead to divorce, and she investigates why, using her own union as an exploratory lens.

Katherine Woodward Thomas, *Conscious Uncoupling: The 5 Steps to Living Happily Even After,* **Hodder & Stoughton, 2015**

The best-selling book on how to carefully craft 'life-affirming' divorces. Made famous by celebrity actress Gwyneth Paltrow, this book focuses on "tender transitions," where each partner works to support each other's best interests in separation. Includes a 'conscious uncoupling creed' that is a good foundational alliance for loving exits.

Sharon Pope, *Why Isn't This Marriage Enough? How to Make Your Marriage Work and Love the Life You Have,* Morgan James Publishing, 2016

I discovered Sharon Pope through a *New York Times* article[21] she wrote for the Modern Love column. A self-defined "love coach," she's written half a dozen books aimed particularly at women unhappy with their relationships. It will give you a deep exploration of every possible question about choosing to leave.

VIDEOS

There are no right and wrong choices, it is simply that the decisions you make (or don't make) will create the path of the rest of your life, and the person you become. These talks explore the challenge of making one of the most important choices of them all.

Ruth Chang, *"How to Make Hard Choices,"* https://www.ted.com/speakers/ruth_chang

Ruth Chang is a philosopher who says that one of the mistakes we make in evaluating tough choices is that we put them on a par with each other. She underlines the reality that choices are difficult is because we try to apply scientific choice lists to values-based decisions. In choice, outcomes are not just better, worse or equal. When values like love are involved, we create reasons for the people we choose to become. It is a choice that is not dictated to us, but invented by us. We then become the authors of our own lives. Who am I to be? If you don't choose, you become a drifter, someone allowing the world to define them. Very empowering talk that kicks you to face up to the gift being offered you with each hard choice.

---

21 Sharon Pope, "Keeping the Boardroom out of the Bedroom" *New York Times,* March 24, 2017 https://www.nytimes.com/2017/03/24/style/modern-love-keeping-the-boardroom-out-of-the-bedroom.html?_r=0

Alain de Botton, *"Why You Will Marry the Wrong Person,"*
https://www.youtube.com/
watch?v=zuKV2DI9-Jg

Alain de Botton is a Swiss-born philosopher who started the School of Life in London. Brilliant, erudite and occasionally infuriating, he is always worth a read. The School of Life has a huge part of its programs focused on love, and de Botton has published two fictional books about couples – one about young love, and the most recent about a middle-aged couple going through a tough time,[22] complete with psychological commentary and analysis. His overriding message is that we are all flawed and need to accept it – both in ourselves and others. I disagree, but it is worth rubbing your own relationship up against his theory. If it convinces you, all the better.

Alain de Botton, *"Stay or Go?"*
https://www.youtube.com/
watch?v=YGV5o6UHjxM

A wonderful acknowledgement of how common the stay or leave choice is in modern marriages. He normalises the choice and some of the issues that so many humans are up against. De Botton's School of Life has been instrumental in presenting the choice as a normal part of life and accompanying people through it. This short clip offers 10 questions to ask yourself as you weigh up the options "between hope and experience." However, de Botton's cynicism about the likelihood of drastically improving your love life seeps through, so be forewarned. He doesn't believe in happy endings. I do.

---

22   Alain de Botton, *The Course of Love*, 2016. Also the earlier and lovelier *Essays in Love*, 1993.

MOVIES

It's still rare in films to see smart, modern women honestly wrestling with mature choices. Thank God for Meryl Streep. These films are both about older couples struggling with divorce and late love. One ends with them staying together, the other with them staying apart. Both end happily.

- *Hope Springs*, Meryl Streep and Tommy Lee Jones
- *It's Complicated*, Meryl Streep, Alec Baldwin, Steve Martin

LOOKING

Loving Anew

"It takes half your life before you discover life is a do-it-yourself project."

Napoleon Hill

"Women like a man with a past, but they prefer a man with a present."

Mae West

BEING, ALONE

· ·

“The chances are high that you may never find anyone else. I have so many friends who have left their husbands and ended up alone, over fifty and lonely,” my friend Cecile told me over a long dinner where I had shared my doubts about my marriage. This, I was to find, would be a dominant theme in many conversations. The spectre of being alone, female and aging was the ultimate fear for many. One friend of mine is panicked by the prospect of being alone, without a man. The attitude and assumptions we bring to the idea of being alone hugely affect this chapter on finding new love. “One is never in a good frame of mind to choose a partner rationally,” writes Alain de Botton, “when remaining single is unbearable.”[23]

The statistics back these visions up. As we have seen, men tend to remarry quickly, while women don’t. But the stereotype of the sad spinster is an exaggeration. Most women have more and closer friends, who are a key support for anyone returning to a single life. More and more older people are cohabiting and choosing not to live alone. Since the majority of Leavers are women, is the reason there are more older unmarried women simply because they are more reluctant to throw themselves

---

23   School of Life, “How We End Up Marrying the Wrong Person”
      http://www.theschooloflife.com/melbourne/blog/2014/07/how-we-end-up-marrying-the-wrong-person/

into another unsatisfactory relationship? Many men are content with their married lot (or less able to function on their own), so it's natural that they want to reproduce the situation they were in when their marriage ends. But women don't.

Leavers and Left have different expectations of subsequent relationships. The Left would like to reproduce what they had, while the Leavers are interested in more and better—or nothing. This distinction is key to your next phase. The end of one thing determines the beginning of the next thing. Trying to digest what has happened, and why, is key to not reproducing the patterns that got you here. Many of the Leavers I spoke with had spent years thinking and analysing their relationships. None of them left lightly. By the time they left, they had usually spent a lot of time trying to figure themselves out, and how they had gotten into a relationship that ended up becoming intolerable. They were usually also clear about what they wanted – and didn't want - from any subsequent relationship. Interestingly, most of them actively wanted another one. The Leavers were decisive in leaving one thing, and equally decisive about finding something else —something different.

FINDING YOURSELF

The best ingredient to finding happiness in late love is to find yourself first. I don't mean going off onto a mountain top in India and staring at your belly button, what the French beautifully refer to as "*nombrilisme*." But I am regularly struck in the executive and leadership coaching I do, by how little people know themselves, where they are headed and what their impact is on others. There are a myriad of tools to help people gain some sense of who they are, what their personality traits mean, how their preferences express themselves and how these differ from others. Unfortunately, this kind of coaching is only offered to a few. There is little of it taught at younger ages and stages, in university and business schools, where it would help in choosing careers, and partners. "Preparing us for marriage is, ideally, an educational task that falls on culture as a whole," advises the London-based

School of Life, but for the moment, we fall woefully short of this ideal. Despite an ever-expanding wedding industry, and a fast-growing couples counselling industry, the real work of learning to love is as yet in its infancy. Learning to love someone else first requires us to know — and love — ourselves.

The author and television writer, Tracy MacMillan, calls this "marrying yourself."[24] In a moving TED talk, this funny and authentic woman sheepishly describes her own repetitive cycling through relationship hell. After three marriages, all of which she left, she looks at herself, "this person with the terrible track record," and asks why would anyone want to marry her? That set her on a journey of self-acceptance. She took the time she never had to be alone, long enough to begin to understand who she was. She describes how she was finally able to take the most solemn of vows with herself: to love the good and the bad, the sick and the healthy, for better or worse. Because if you don't, no one else is likely to want to either. Her story moved me – and probably the two million other people who watched it – to tears.

For a full explanatory exercise self reflection, check out Loving Bravely. It will take you to each of four steps:

1. self-reflection

2. self-awareness

3. self-expression

4. self-expansion.

The guiding principle of this book and this chapter is an invitation to become "relationally self-aware."[25]

---

24   TED Talk https://www.youtube.com/watch?v=P3fIZuW9P_M&nohtml5=False

25   Alexandra Solomon and Mona Fishbane, *Loving Bravely,* 2017.

Lost

David Wagoner

Stand still. The trees ahead and bushes beside you

Are not lost. Wherever you are is called Here,

And you must treat it as a powerful stranger,

Must ask permission to know it and be known.

The forest breathes. Listen. It answers,

I have made this place around you.

If you leave it, you may come back again, saying Here.

No two trees are the same to Raven.

No two branches are the same to Wren.

If what a tree or a bush does is lost on you,

You are surely lost. Stand still. The forest knows

Where you are. You must let it find you.

Self-awareness is no easy task. While age plays a part in self-understanding, it is no guarantee. Life is an education, but learning is optional. As Harville Hendrix has written, "Marriage is not a static state between two unchanging people. Marriage is a psychological and spiritual journey that begins in the ecstasy of attraction, meanders through a rocky stretch of self-discovery, and culminates in the creation of an intimate, joyful, lifelong union. Whether you realize the full potential of this vision depends not on your ability to attract the perfect mate, but on your willingness to acquire knowledge about hidden parts of yourself."[26] He suggests that people find mates who represent the part of themselves they seek to reinforce or engage with. So people who have unresolved issues or wounds from childhood often end up marrying a person who evokes the parent with whom they are seeking resolution.

This is what happened to David. "Two years into my first marriage, I heard myself say: 'Holy God, I've married my father!'" David had been brought up with a model of mother as caretaker and father as taker. He twice married a taker, until he finally learned that the dark side of his own caretaking was control. "It was an illness on both sides, we were both emotionally ill and damaged. And for two decades I thought that if I could just become more conscious and compassionate, then maybe love would come my way. I had two completely co-dependent relationships, each grounded in the same pattern of 'I give, you take'." The watershed moment finally came when David had done enough soul-searching and growing and got to a point where, for the first time in his life, he was no longer afraid of being alone. "I learned that nothing changes until you do. Humans have such a capacity to love, if we could only start to do it with ourselves. That's the doorway, and the key."

WHO CHANGES?

One of the challenges of this voyage of discovery inside marriage is that it requires two willing, curious tourists. Both partners need to want to travel, or at least be ready to go along for the ride. Too often, one person feels dragged along by the other, and made to feel as though they are a problem that requires resolving.

---

26   Harville Hendrix, *Getting the Love You Want,* Simon & Schuster, 1988

Overwhelmingly, it is wives who bring their husbands for counselling or coaching, says Sue Saker, a London-based, ORSC-trained[27] relationship coach. "It's much harder to get the guys interested. I speak to a lot of women who say, 'I would love to do it but there is no way my husband would even consider it.' Yet if they come, they love it. There is an imbalance between men and women's communication skills around emotions. Often women do a lot of talking and dominating, so you need to work to give the men some air time. They take a bit more time to express themselves. And they fear that I will side with their wives. But in coaching sessions, the men suddenly have a voice, they actually get to say what they are feeling and be heard. A light bulb goes off."

Most women revel in the relationship stuff, and most men do not. Are we doomed then to this stalemate of women yearning and men resisting? I think the problem may be partly one of tone and context. Men are discovering that modern marriage is more like the modern workplace than they thought. It isn't for life, and your spouse can quit even if you are saying everything is fine. Women may want to learn how to frame their invitation to deepen the ties that bind into a more attractive proposition. One of the best ways to do this is to begin the conversation before the conflicts. Suddenly demanding a change in the rules of the game halfway through life just doesn't land very well.

Many men feel their partners are trying to change them, rather than changing the relationship. While one partner may feel they are inviting the other on a delightful journey of mutual self-exploration and self-discovery, the other may feel judged and defensive – and slam on the brakes. But through my professional experience I have worked with many men who appreciatively learn and grow from self-understanding. Leadership coaching is all about knowing yourself and your impact on others. People I coached didn't change into something they weren't; they became more consciously and powerfully themselves.

---

27 ORSC, Organisation and Relationship Systems Coaching. A coaching approach that focuses on systems (the relationship) rather than individuals. I followed this programme in 2015.

I had trouble understanding that someone might not be as interested in learning about themselves as I was. Yet it's true that in companies, executives aren't asked to do this work, they're told to – and then they tell me that they have discovered, much to their own surprise, that it has been helpful and impactful. But getting the order from your wife just doesn't go down as well. Leadership in our complex, global, fast-changing world of work takes a steady, skilled human mind and heart. The same is true at home. We all need skills to manage relationships, and the more intimate they are, the more complex they become.

Learning to love yourself and others requires knowing who you are talking about. We all have a myriad of selves and dimensions we've barely explored. The less we know ourselves, the more these hidden facets are likely to surface and speak in our stead, disrupting our relationships and lives in a variety of ways we are largely unconscious of.

"To love without knowing how to love wounds the person we love."

Zen teacher *Thich Nhat Hanh*

Looking back, it seems to me that we are all desperately unskilled. Despite often years of efforts, I, and so many other women, find we are not getting through to our mates, a frustration captured in the title of Terry Real's wonderful book on intimacy gaps between men and women, *How Can I Get Through to You?*[28] I think we should admit some share of the responsibility. I do. Because we are often operating from a place that is wounded and hurt and disappointed, it is hard to keep the invitation to dance light and seductive. More often, I'm sure we come across as accusing, embittered and dissatisfied.

---

28   Terrence Real, *How Can I Get Through To You? Closing the Intimacy Gap Between Men and Women,* Simon & Schuster, 2003

"Men don't feel things in the same way," says Saker. "For them, relationships are not such a big deal, and not at the forefront of their minds. Things are OK. If it isn't really unpleasant, if it's just OK, they assume this is normal. The wife is working and questioning to make it better. The reality is that often these relationships are far less satisfying than both make them out to be." If you want to improve a relationship, she says, you need to focus on it.

Why is it that some people and some relationships age and become wiser and deeper and more mature, while others just age? What's the difference? Awareness.

Love After Love
Derek Walcott

The time will come

when, with elation,

you will greet yourself arriving

at your own door, in your own mirror,

and each will smile at the other's welcome,

and say, sit here. Eat.

You will love again the stranger who was your self.

Give wine. Give bread. Give back your heart

to itself, to the stranger who has loved you

all your life, whom you ignored

for another, who knows you by heart.

Take down the love letters from the bookshelf,

the photographs, the desperate notes,

peel your own image from the mirror.

Sit. Feast on your life.

"Who does ever get what they want?" asks Kent Haruf in his last novel about a late love couple, *Our Souls at Night*.[29] "It doesn't seem to happen to many of us if any at all. It's always two people bumping against each other blindly, acting out of old ideas and dreams and mistaken understandings."

As Vincent Deary has written in his brilliant book *How to Live*, we are, more than we like to admit, a collection of largely unconscious patterns. These patterns are hugely influenced by our parents and our own upbringing. The only way to change patterns is to become conscious of them. His book is a step-by-step guide to change. Change sweeps in and disrupts our patterns, and then we adapt, and, eventually, go about "re-saming" or re-establishing new patterns for new circumstances. This can be done consciously and intentionally, or it can happen *to* you.

Robert is a good example of how a search for self-knowledge leads to change. He is an accountant, and literally let the numbers rule his life. He was born into a "poor, unhappy, working-class" home in the 50s, in a world he says was totally different. "Today, young people think they can do anything. Then, we thought we could do nothing." When he went to university, his simple dorm room felt extraordinarily luxurious. "Many people go into accountancy," he admits, "because of poverty in their own childhoods" so they can control their financial fears in adulthood. His earliest relationships were marked by abandonment. His parents died suddenly in a car crash when he was 25, and his undigested grief led him to marry soon after, a woman he now sees "should have stayed a friend." Within a decade, she left him for a man she met at work. At 50, after a series of relationships had petered out listlessly, he decided to look inwards. He went to a series of Gestalt groups, and then, spurred on by a friend, to a 9-month self-development program run by Darren Eden at the Academy of Greatness.[30] He was, he says, successful in every area of life—except intimacy. "I had an illusion of freedom, because I had chosen to live in a rather small bubble," he discovered. In a gradual process

---

29 Kent Haruf, *Our Souls at Night,* Picador, 2016
30 http://www.academyofgreatness.co.uk/Your_Call_To_Greatness.html

of opening up and revisiting who he thought he was, he made a new group of friends. He wouldn't know it until much later, but his late love was among them.

Can we become masterful at love? The answer seems related to so much of the work I do professionally. There are leaders who become masterful at relationships with people, and others who don't. And the same qualities and lessons that infuse people's ability to inspire, motivate and work with others at work seem directly related to how able we are to inspire, motivate and love our partners, our families and ourselves. Yet the starting point in all this work is the same. Do we understand ourselves?

Mastery involves focused, repetitive practice. In Malcolm Gladwell's famous telling of it,[31] true masters are not born, they have invested 10,000 hours in their crafts. The same is true of relationships—with ourselves and others. Once we have invested the thought and the time and the practice, we can hope to become masters of ourselves, and masterful in relating to others. Until then, we are all amateurs in the rollicking roller coaster of life and love. So we need to ask ourselves some questions, and give the responses serious thought.

- Do we understand how others see us?
- Do we know our impact on others? Have we asked?
- Do we have a vision of where we want to go, and are we able to inspire others to share the journey to get there?
- Are we able to listen – and hear both the message and the emotion that surrounds it?
- Are we able to express and get what we need?
- Can/do we give others what they need? Do we know what that is?

Can we build the skills to be better at love? Much of the advice and guidelines for leadership at work are directly transferable to those who would like to be better leaders of their own lives and loves.

---

31   Malcolm Gladwell, *Outliers: The Story of Success,* Penguin, 2008

Leaders across the world are dropping command and control styles of the past because it doesn't work well with today's knowledge workers. Turns out, it doesn't work so well at home either. At work, leaders are being coached to become more collaborative, more skilled at conflict resolution and more able to listen and work inclusively across human differences of all kinds. All of these skills are hugely useful at home too.

Some of the marriage advice being doled out by research on long-term married couples seems to have too strong an attachment to the idea that staying together is the superior outcome. Rather than exploring what's going on, and whether or not there are two people ready to work together, a lot of advice seems to be more directed towards conflict avoidance, acceptance of things as they are, and a recommendation to settle for "good enough." This seems contrary to the very human search for personal enlightenment and peace. Why would we be so intent on developing people's capacity for leadership at work, and spend so little time on our capacities for relationship enlightenment and leadership in the crucial dimensions of personal life? The challenges of modern romance, fuelled by shifting gender roles and accelerated by technological revolutions and generational shifts in attitudes, make these skills urgently needed.

While many people in search of love throw themselves into online dating and matching sites, a more effective first step is to look inside. Finding a good mate requires becoming one yourself. That means knowing yourself—intimately. What are your patterns? Your history with family, with relationships, with work? With yourself? Are you aware of the part you have played in all these stories, and have you accepted your share of the responsibility for both the successes and failures? What are your goals, not just in love, but in life? Have you learned to accept who you are and where you have arrived? Are you looking for a partner to make you whole, or someone with whom to celebrate your wholeness?

It took David into his 60s to come to terms with being alone. "I had finally come to the point of self-love and self-esteem where I didn't need another person to complete me." And that, of course, is the moment he was finally ready to meet his late love. Richard put up with a difficult, dependent wife in a deeply unhappy marriage for 30 years. Now, he wonders why he waited so long. One day, at age 58, three days after meeting Marie at a hotel where he was staying for a medical conference, he threw all his clothes in a car, moved to her town and declared he was marrying her... it took him a couple of years, but now, a decade later, he admits that "just being with a happy, successful person changed my life."

I spent about a decade – most of my 40s – on this. I certified as a coach back in 2000, and found it helpful in navigating through the challenges of one of life's most intense decades. The 40s saw my children become teenagers, my mother and in-laws fall ill, family members dying, at the same time both my and my husband's careers growing and becoming increasingly time-consuming and travel-heavy. It was non-stop on all fronts. Regular thinking, writing and goal-setting became survival strategies. My journal was both memory bank and free shrink. As an extrovert, I know I figure things out through writing and talking. I did a lot of both in these years. Both calmed me down, and often allowed me to take the role of observer in my own life. A little less reaction, and a bit more analysis. They also allowed me to plan, and pace myself. Conscious self-reflection eventually allowed me to fall in love... with me.

Despite the appearance of being an easy and relaxed person, I had always been fairly hard on myself. I was a seriously self-hating teenager—overweight, a bit too assertive, a complete misfit in the calm Anglo part of Toronto I grew up in. My brilliant older brother was consistently condescending, and I internalized a good part of his disdain. Like many people, the critical voices in my head were extremely loud for much of the first half of my life. A grudging self-acceptance came with the years, and the exploration, and the dawning realization that most people share a generalized discomfort with life and existence.

As a coach, I've done a myriad of tests, analyses and 360 feedback exercises. There is a vast range of self-analysis tools out there, but a few basic ones should give you a pretty good picture of some of your key personality traits. They are listed in the Toolkit at the end of this chapter. The personality test Helen Fisher developed for Match.com, and the Enneagram, are good places to start. If you are, or have been, in relationships with people of different nationalities, I recommend throwing in the cross-cultural self-test from Geert Hofstede's work on nationality profiles. And if you are in a heterosexual couple, I think some education on gender differences is essential for both partners. A good place to begin is Deborah Tannen's work on differences in communications styles (see books listed in the Toolkit section).

While self-analysis is a great starting point, in fine-tuning relationship skills it's important to get a sense of your impact on other people. The key point of feedback exercises is to check whether your self-image has any actual relationship to reality. If the story you are telling yourself about yourself isn't true, you are unlikely to find relationships easy to build, and hard to maintain.

It also seems, from the research from big online dating sites, what people think they want is not actually what they go for. It's hard if you don't have an accurate picture of yourself, to be able to formulate—and sometimes even imagine—what you may be after in a mate for the second half of your life. Will you mostly be running as far as you can from the negative characteristics you found in previous relationships, or what you felt was missing, what I call designing "From" relationships? Will you simply be projecting your needs onto another person and mistakenly assume you are made for each other? I received a very funny card that summarises this beautifully. A fat cat on the front generously declares: "I will love you just the way I am." Alternatively, will you have a deeper understanding of the key drivers that motivate you, your own vulnerabilities, triggers, strengths and be as fully "self-actualized" as possible so that a late relationship becomes an additional "cherry on the cake," rounding out a rounded life? This is what I call a "To" relationship. Where you are ready to discover and love someone as they are, not so much as they reflect your needs.

It seems we are lousy predictors of what will make us happy. My late love Tim has said I am in so many ways the opposite of any of the women he had ever dated. Robert ended up falling for Helena a year after meeting her, and only after they had haphazardly been thrown together for an evening, and stayed up talking until dawn. "She ticked none of the boxes I might have unconsciously had about potential partners." Kathleen ended up with a quiet, supportive nuclear engineer, who didn't look or feel anything like the kind of men she thought she wanted. A quick look at Dan Ariely's work on irrationality[32] only confirms that, consistently throughout our lives, we are not serving our own long-term interests. We have no idea what they are.

It comes down to Maslow's old hierarchy of needs (see below). If you are lucky, and live in a developed country, you were born into the first couple of levels where security and food were taken as given. Then you spend the rest of your life, moving up through the rest of the menu: from material possessions through professional success and recognition. As people age, and particularly in the latter third of life, some of this journey has been done, and people graduate to an interest in more metaphysical matters: self-knowledge, spirituality, giving back to others in some way. It seems to me that one of the essential success factors for couples is to be at a similar level of this hierarchy, and of self-awareness in general. If both halves of a couple are steeped in materialism, or in metaphysical pursuits, it can work. But trying to live with someone at a very different place on their own life journey is difficult. It's not differences in people that hurt as much as living with a very different purpose from your partner, and a very different level of awareness about what any of this even means.

Another way of expressing this is made even more visible in one of the personality tests I recommend, from the Enneagram Institute. Within each of the nine *types* of people this test outlines, there are also nine *levels* of self-awareness and development, from the unhealthy Level 1, to the highly evolved Level 9. Each level is slightly more evolved along a spectrum of unhealthy, average to healthy levels.

---

32   Dan Ariely, *Predictably Irrational: The Hidden Forces that Shape Our Decisions,* HarperCollins, revised edition 2010

MASLOW'S HIERARCHY OF HUMAN NEEDS

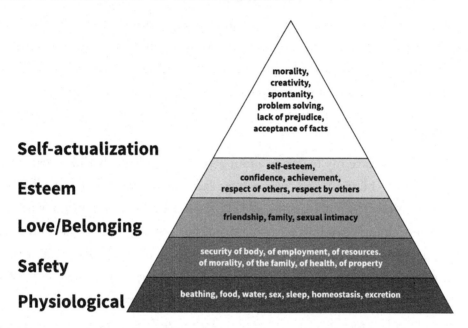

You can, like me and like Robert, throw yourself into self-development courses or one of the myriad of different self-development approaches out there. Or, more simply, check out what The School of Life has to offer, in their range of short evening courses their vast library of relevant online videos about love. You can also just go around to friends and colleagues and ask for a bit of honest, structured feedback.

It's worth it. David now basks, finally, in contentment, with Elisabeth and with himself. "I've never had so much joy. It started with love of self. People shy away from this because they see it as selfish. But narcissism is based in self-loathing, and you can't love someone else if you don't love yourself."

ON LOOKING, AND FINDING, A MATCH

As I said in the last chapter, I made lots of mistakes in my journey. I was prepared, and I had a high level of self-awareness both of why I needed to leave and what I wanted to move towards. But I didn't sufficiently prepare many of those most affected by my decision. And, as you'll see, in one important way I was either a coward or pretty selfish, in that I didn't want to leave before actually having found what I was looking for. Here I'm going to tell you my story, for both the good and the less good lessons it contains.

I had finally decided to leave my marriage about a year before I finally did. There were all kinds of reasons, of course. The children's ages were a huge factor, with the eldest just off to college, the youngest three years behind. The build-up of failed efforts to rekindle a relationship with my husband was another. In the end, though, symbols pushed me out the door. New Year's Day of the year I would turn 50, I turned to a good friend and announced this would be the year I left my marriage. I'm not a big believer in numbers and big birthdays. But I couldn't bear going on, in a state of suspended dissatisfaction, across the threshold of another decade, and into the second half of my life.

Saying it out loud made it real. And kicked that reality to life. The power of the spoken word. But it was actually the second step of a journey that had begun the day before.

I had been vaguely looking around my world for a year or two, in a purely hypothetical way. At other men, at dating sites, at my friends. What would I find, I wondered, as I stepped outside of the protected enclave of my suburban mom's experience? Would it be the lovelorn desert some spoke of, or the predatory jungle of desperation? Would I be one of millions of aging women longing for some fantasy of a soul-mate?

In the end, I never found out. I didn't throw myself into the fray. Instead, I propositioned an old friend. A group of my oldest friends were hanging out at our house before our annual New Year's Eve dinner celebration. Two of my very favourite friends, both lifelong singles, were sitting on the couch across from me. Tim was showing Jo his brand-new, just-launched iPad, by flipping through his photo gallery. I was familiar with much of what he was sharing, but as he narrated his life, I found my attention increasingly drawn to the couch. I had always known Tim as a kind, rather earnest, intellectual type. Now I started to discover other aspects of his personality. He showed his sculptures first. Gorgeous works he had created in wood and bronze, most of them glorious odes to womanhood, sinuous, sensuous portraits of adoration. Then he started showing pictures of his home, a 200-year-old Georgian thing he had spent a decade almost single-handedly renovating into glorious minimalist modernism. Next were the photos of the 120-year old steamboat he and his father had spent another decade renovating, piece by historical piece, in a shared delight in boats and each other's company.

I could almost see my unconscious check list for new love being ticked off one item at a time: must love women, must go deep, must have good relationships with parents. First, a love of women was key. I desperately wanted a man who loved women—in all their wise and wonderful glory. I didn't just want to be amicably loved as an equal. I was tired of unsexy and undifferentiated egalitarianism. I wanted to be adored and admired as a representative of something mysteriously and divinely different. And here was a man who had spent years sculpting every rounded curve and hillock in obvious exultation.

I also love good taste and design and art. A strong aesthetic taste, displayed not only externally in his (I must admit) handsome form, but also liberally on view in his seriously chic London home and garden. Every detail of the whole was carefully designed and thought through. He also loved books (with a romantic's penchant for Jane Austen), music, film and long intellectual discussions. The ultimate sensitive man…

And finally, his lovely relationship with his father was inspiring (his mother had died some 20 years earlier). I had come to agree with my friend Marian that parental relationships are a key indicator of partnership preparedness. The ability to forge deep, profound and committed ties with a partner depends to no mean extent on whether you have developed such ties with other humans. Much ink has been spilled on this point. It's as true in kittens and puppies as it is in humans. Coming from good, loving parents sets you up with the default skills to be a good, loving partner. You can, of course, acquire these even if you weren't the lucky beneficiary of them at birth. But this takes a huge amount of work on yourself—something that most people just don't do. Good relationships with parents—especially mothers—seems a pre-condition to good relationships. And there was Tim, right before me, explaining that he had spent a decade with his 90-year-old dad contentedly entranced by their joint passion.

At this point, it was a little bit like lightning had struck. "Tim!" I thought to myself. "Of course, Tim!" I was suddenly speechless. Jo told me later I was staring rather too intently ... I wouldn't have to go trawling the Internet or wandering around singles' bars. I wouldn't have to go live alone to prove I was a modern woman and could be entirely self-sufficient. Right here in front of me was a fine specimen of a man. He also happened to be a very dear old friend and confidant of some quarter of a century.

And, icing on the cake, he was—and had always been—single. I'd tried to set him up often enough with a variety of friends of mine over the years. I never quite understood why such an unusually eligible bachelor had stayed single, though I was about to find out.

Of course, there was also a fly in the ointment. He was not only my friend, but also my husband's. The kindness and basic decency that made him a valued friend also made him an unlikely solution to my search. Not to mention the detail that he lived in a different country – I was in France, he was in the UK.

He, and all our other friends, left a couple of days later. I remember my then husband and I taking Jo and Tim into Paris for dinner before they caught their Eurostar back to London. As they left, I could almost feel my heart stretching out after them, pulling away from me. My favourite friends were leaving, and I was left behind with someone I didn't want to be with… *There is something deeply wrong with this picture*, I thought. It was, I decided, time to act.

The next day was Monday January 3. And that morning, before getting to work on another year of busyness, I screwed up all my courage and my resolve, and wrote this missive to Tim:

Dear Tim,

OK, so one of my new year's resolutions is to show more vulnerability. So, this email is a leap in that direction. Please be gentle.

The real work of this next phase is extricating myself, nicely, from my marriage. I realize I'm having trouble doing this alone, and need some help. It occurred to me this past weekend, you might be just the man for the task… (This is where I feel your jaw dropping.)

This partnership has run its course; it is not a catastrophe, nor is it deeply unhappy, it is just simply, dully, unfulfilling. For both of us, I think; I know I am not getting what I need, and I fear I am actually not at all good for my husband. I could go on, but that should suffice. I have spent years trying to 'work' at this as they say, without almost any progress at all.

I do not AT ALL underestimate the pain that this will cause, which is why it is taking me so long to act. One of the reasons for procrastination is that it isn't so awful that I feel an urgent need to cause pain if there is no commensurate pleasure for anyone involved. I don't feel I can leave just for leaving, I feel I need to leave FOR something - or someone. That's where you come in (this is not easy).

You've long been a friend, and always someone I could talk to. Despairingly, more easily than my own husband. I was struck these past few days by how much so much of what you say, do and dream resonates with me. The idealism, the skepticism, the ardor, the intelligence and the kindness you inhabit so completely and authentically. Funnily, you make me feel at home. I literally felt like leaning up next to you and had to remind myself that this wasn't acceptable behavior for the married hostess.…

So, this is a proposal to explore. (Really, I would prefer to have the gentleman make the first move, but understand that in the current circumstances this would not make him a gentleman…)

I have no idea where you are with your heart. And maybe all your considerable perfectionism will stop this idea dead in its tracks. Or maybe you are now content with your way of life. Or, or, or… interesting that I know so much more about your professional musings than your personal ones… but then I'm not forgetting you're British…

Even writing this is deeply, deeply awkward. I'm cringing and pushing myself through this. So if you are totally embarrassed and want to hide under the bed, you will have my total empathy. But at our ages and stages, I think embarrassment and hesitation will, quite literally, be the death of us. So I'm picking up your New Year's resolution to dare more.

And, if you see, as I do, the glimmer of a possibility of a connection that might actually work, after all the initial awkwardness, pain, pleasure, discovery and change is over, let's do dinner. The only answer required is a simple yes or no. If no, we'll never speak of this again, continue as the friends I hope we long will be, and I know I can count on your complete discretion. I was going to let this email sit in drafts for a day, but then I think I would not send it. So it will go off now, and since you are on vacation, you'll have the time to mull over it at your leisure, and I will go off to work, in thanks for having done something.

In appreciation for the compassion with which I know you have just read these lines.

A

Now, I'm not proud of this. I'm sure many will feel that I should have formally broken up with my husband before acting. I even agree with you. But for some reason, I felt strongly that I just wasn't interested in tearing apart my family and creating a lot of pain for nothing. While I wasn't happy, my marriage wasn't so awful that anyone was getting hurt. I wasn't desperate or in any immediate hurry. I wanted more—more love and emotional involvement and sharing—not less. The idea of wreaking havoc to be alone just wasn't a trade-off I was ready to make. I felt like I had been alone for a long time. My exit strategy demanded a partner. It needed a destination.

I wasn't so much running away from my marriage, as many of the people I interviewed were, almost as a condition of survival. I was running "to" love, and that required finding it first. And testing that it was true. I felt I had signalled my unhappiness to my husband, over several years, in things said, letters written and attempts at couples coaching. But these were attempts to *save* our marriage - not prepare him for its ending. I conflated two stages: the attempt to repair and the declaration of an ending.

Needless to say, Tim was totally stunned by my email out of nowhere. He first wanted to help save our marriage, and it took several exchanges to convince him that, whatever his own decision, mine to leave my husband was definitive. He was saddened by the loss of the picture he had of my family. But I made it clear that continuing the status quo was no longer an option.

In doing so I presented him with one of the most difficult decisions in life. At 55 and still single after several unsuccessful attempts at relationships, he still believed in love – yet had largely come to accept that somehow it had passed him by. Now I offered him a late chance, but one that required him to choose between two very old friends – and hurt one of them. I am sorry for my husband and I am sorry for Tim – and yet not sorry, because he did choose. He faced the issue and, like me, opted for love and away from loneliness. Put like that it may seem obvious, but for him too, it was the hardest and most painful decision he ever took.

Living in different countries turned out to be a blessing; we spent the next few weeks writing daily letters to each other. Exploring, debating, discovering, increasingly intimate, searingly honest, they launched us on a journey from very old, good friends to mature and mutually supportive mates. I discovered the reason behind his singlehood. The black cloud of depression had over-shadowed much of his adult life, and hampered his ability to reach out for another. Decades of the ups and downs of real depression, a disease I knew little about at the time, had undercut this man's life. It had also, eventually, and late in life, blessed him with a deep self-knowledge and a compassion for other's suffering that I found rare and welcoming. The wrinkles of his long-suffering face are – astonishingly - imbued with love. I didn't know what I was really getting into, but I was not afraid of pain.

My own family's history was suffused with it. It sticks to the genes through generations. Humans seem to learn some degree of humanity through suffering. My mother models grace, humour and love after surviving Auschwitz as a young woman. She then lost her beloved husband to cancer as a young wife and mother in a strange country, Canada, to which they had emigrated. Her experience has imprinted the depths of my soul. I grew up intimately aware of evil and darkness, and its global reach and constant presence. There was never much innocence in the deeper reaches. Victims of all kinds are usually much more awake to the world than their oppressors, and more empathetic to human frailty.

I think our respective psychic darkness spoke as much to each other as our determined smiles did. We were old, and deep, and unafraid. Our intimacy with these realities made us strong. It also contextualised what we were doing. In the grand scheme of history, we were reaching out in love, not hate. We would love more and better together than we could apart. We felt fully seen for the first time. It was heady, brutally honest and uncompromisingly real.

It was also revelatory. We were old, old friends. Yet I had no idea what he had gone through for so many years. I was humbled. And relieved, like tumbling into something unexpectedly warm and welcoming. Deepening an existing relationship is an equal mix of familiarity and surprise. This was not some kind of passionate physical attraction. It was all by email! It was recognition. It reminded me of birdsong. The way birds sing out in mating, and then hear a matching call that echoes their tune. I suddenly heard my own song sung by another soul. There is no sound more deeply comforting in all the world. It bids loneliness goodbye and ushers you into the land of an aliveness that has not left me since.

A month later, I told my husband I was leaving.

I'm hardly recommending this as a strategy. It's not fair to your existing partner, I know. It's not even fair to the old friend, if you take that route. But it is not that unusual. Couples know when there is something wrong with their couple. You either acknowledge the issues and deal with them, or you can be guaranteed that one of the two will be preparing their exit. The challenge is that often, and certainly in my case, one partner is preparing their exit, while the other denies that there is anything wrong.

If you feel your partner is unhappy, or your relationship is at risk, address it. Talk, write, share, find a way to explore the gap. *Both* halves of a couple are responsible for any split. Not just the one walking out the door. Although that is certainly the image many of those left behind then do their best to communicate: that of a victim who really had no idea why their partner left, or that there was anything wrong at all. This has always struck me as slightly ludicrous. It is a strange relationship where one partner is unhappy enough to leave while the other claims obliviousness to any trouble. While Leavers may be the one to walk, most often it is because the partner left behind either wouldn't acknowledge the problem or refused to engage in finding a solution.

Leavers get the rap, and the Left are seen as victims. When Nina left, she admitted that she had to gear herself up to the judgments she felt she would be subject to. "I felt that I would have to cope with the stereotypes people associate with the person initiating a divorce. That they are hard, uncompromising, ungiving, self-centred and non-nurturing. This is not the person I wanted to be. It takes a lot to test the waters, and hope that people will still see me as me."

Lisa left her first, philandering husband she married at 20 as soon as she got a promotion at work and had enough money to leave with her two children. "I was the first person in my (traditional, Jewish) family to get divorced. My parents didn't speak to me for six months. My father apologised for that on his deathbed." But for Lisa, it was liberating. "I was asserting myself."

While my approach may not be exactly kosher, I must admit it was, at least for me, comforting, exciting and hugely facilitated the transition I was dreaming of. Many people who leave a spouse end up with a friend. And it seems these relationships are more likely to last. It makes sense. Building a relationship with someone with whom you already have a long history removes a lot of risk. There is an immediate sense of trust, and shared history. While the initial shock for children is probably greater with someone they know as a family friend, in the longer term, the fact that this person is familiar and knows them from an early age contributes to their eventual closeness.

Robert was a Presbyterian minister who had married a graduate student from the same seminary. They both were gifted in their fields and did well in the church. But he knew (or now admits should have known) right from his honeymoon that something was wrong when he found himself reading the sports pages for something to do. This led to a passionless, 20-year marriage of separate bedrooms and some despair. "It was hard as a pastor leaning into the concept of divorce. I had two therapists, and when I finally said the word, I knew I was doing what I had to do. I also knew that if I left my wife, I'd also have to leave the church I had served for 27 years…" It was to set him on a whole new path, personally and professionally.

Take a look at your existing social network, with new eyes. I would never have dreamt of Tim for myself, not in a million years. Until the day I did, and it seemed so obvious that I laughed at my blindness. It really was like a lightning bolt. Tim never once looked at me in that way, either. I heard the same story from a gay couple I interviewed. Nancy and Marie were both trying to extricate themselves from bad relationships. Nancy adored Marie and was trying to set her up with several of her friends, (just as I had so often tried to set Tim up with others) telling them that Maria was a most extraordinary woman. Until one day, a friend replied, "Then why isn't she for you?" And the scales dropped from her eyes. Why indeed? Today, they have been together for almost 30 years, co-parenting a large extended family of children and grandchildren. I can't explain either the blindness, or the sudden sense of "seeing" someone, as if for the first time.

Marc and Lisa were friends in junior high school. Marc married Lisa's best friend, and when Lisa remarried (after having left philandering husband, see earlier), the resulting two couples remained best friends for decades. Marc lost his wife to lung cancer after 40 happy years. When Lisa's husband died, her kids automatically called on Marc to step in and support her. Three months after his death, Lisa lectured Marc, standing in her kitchen, "You want to get married but you won't be able to find anyone if you spend all your time with me." He simply responded, "I already found her." They started dating officially a couple of months later.

Robert invited a few friends he had made in a self-development program he attended to a concert he was sponsoring. A group of them made the trip down to Brighton. Helena had called him to see if she could stay with him after the concert. They lingered over a post-dinner drink and ended up talking until dawn. And that was it. He says it was literally as though he had been "hit by Cupid's arrow." From someone he had never considered, a bit of happenstance transformed her into the only person he could consider.

Richard was a sudden widower at 58 after 34 years of a happy marriage. He was fragile and admits "the ladies that were thrown at me scared the crap out of me. The newly divorced women were so damn bitter, and some who were single were so charged up it was scary. I hadn't been on the dating scene for 34 years." When a good friend of his late wife remarried at 88 years old, Richard offered her a round of golf for four. She brought Jenn along. Jenn was a long-term single whose motto had been "he has to be an awfully good man, or I'd rather have no man at all." Both were passionately involved in coaching youth sports. After running after a slot in Jenn's over-brimming agenda for weeks, Richard saw her show up for their first real date in a soccer uniform. He immediately thought: "I could marry this person. It scared me a bit."

I find this sudden unlocking or shift in the way we look at someone fascinating. The metaphors of being "hit" with lightning bolts or arrows or insights, give an indication of the size of the flip in the way we see someone. A feeling of intense recognition, or a re-alignment of energies, as if you were really seeing the whole person for the first time.

The psychologists say you have been dreaming your future partner into existence before you meet them. "It is as if, oddly, you were waiting for someone but you didn't know who they were until they arrived. Whether you were aware that there was someone missing in your life, you will be when you meet the person you want. What psychoanalysis adds to this love story is that the person you fall in love with literally *is* the man or woman of your dreams; that you have dreamed them up before you met them... you recognise them with such certainty because you already, in a certain sense, know them; and because you have quite literally been expecting them, you feel as though you have known them forever...[33]

Elisabeth actively dreamt up her man. She spent months after leaving her second husband designing her future. She wrote about it, explored it, dreamt it. "I want to write about the love of man," she wrote in an unpublished essay she shared with me," – not mankind – but a man, a romantic partner. A breathing, living, sexual, thinking, conscious man who has his own life to live. I want to intersect with that person – in more ways than one. This feels like a wilderness. It is definitely vulnerability. I can feel my heart pumping just with the thought of this. I can feel that I am waking up. I want to

---

33 Adam Phillips, *Missing Out: In Praise of the Unlived Life*, Penguin, 2013

wake up. Sleeping beauty has had enough of her beauty sleep. I know that this waking up means you have to get out of bed – the bed where you can pull the covers up over your head. No worries, you can always return there for rest."

She had a huge tree-like drawing in her dining room, where she experimented with visioning different parts of her future life into being. It changed over the course of time, but she started having repetitive dreams of a man walking towards her out of the lake, holding a bouquet of flowers. When one day she opened the door to David, who also lived on her lake, and who was standing holding an orchid on her doorstep, there was that shock of recognition. "You're in trouble now, Elisabeth," she remembers telling herself, immediately.

Poets, like David Whyte, suggest that "longing has its own secret, future destination, and its own seasonal emergence from within, a ripening from the core, a seed growing in our own bodies; it is as if we are put into relationship with an enormous distance inside us leading back to some unknown origin with its own secret timing indifferent to our wills, and gifted at the same time with an intimate sense of proximity, to a lover, to a future, to a transformation, to a life we want for ourselves, and to the beauty of the sky and the ground that surrounds us."[34]

Sometimes, the way we see others is loaded with the limits, assumptions and judgments we carry over from an earlier time, when the person in question may have been different, less evolved, not right for you. Or you simply hadn't had an opportunity to connect beyond the superficial. Of course, it is also true that most people in contented couples simply don't look at other people that way. I know I never did. Not until I had really decided my marriage was terminally impaired did I ever begin to look at other men.

I often think Tim and I would not have been attracted to each other a quarter of a century earlier, although we were already friends. We have aged into different, wiser and more relaxed people

---

34   David Whyte, *Consolations: The Solace, Nourishment and Underlying Meaning of Everyday Words*, Many Rivers Press, 2015

who "fit" together incredibly well. But I think we come from a spectrum that would have been uncomfortably far apart. Nor do I think we necessarily would have been compatible during the more stressful parenting and career-oriented decades. We have grown toward each other, over the intervening time. We have watched our respective evolutions, and love what we have become.

It feels a bit like waking from a midsummer night's dream. You can't quite believe that nothing and everything has changed, as if by a magic wand. After a moment wondering about your sanity, you are left with the consequences of new sight. This is beautifully described in Kent Haruf's novel, *Our Souls at Night*. The book opens with 70-year-old widow Addie Moore walking down the block to her neighbor's house and proposing to Louis that he come and companionably share her bed. Her devil-may-care courage, and his complete but contained shock, provides a perfect replica of my own experience. "I made up my mind I'm not going to pay attention to what people think. I've done that too long – all my life. I'm not going to live that way anymore."[35]

It took all the courage in my heart to sit down and write to Tim. Mixed emotions swirled. I simultaneously winced and shivered all the way through writing it, deeply embarrassed and steeling myself for his probable rejection. But at the same time, it was a huge act of liberation. I had finally moved. After years of debate and inner struggle, with my foot hesitating between the brake and the accelerator, I had finally changed gears and set off down my chosen fork in the road.

---

35   Kent Haruf, *Our Souls at Night,* Picador, 2015

"I shall be telling this with a sigh
Somewhere ages and ages hence:
Two roads diverged in a wood, and I—
I took the one less travelled by,
And that has made all the difference."

Robert Frost

Whatever his answer, publicly declaring my intention to someone made it real. I was on my way… finally choosing to choose. It came as an immense relief. After hitting the send button, I felt freed – by my own hand. And unbeknownst to me, I had simultaneously unlocked an enormous brake in another person's heart. From there, we tumbled into a long—and as yet unending—conversation. Again, just like Haruf's book, it started with a lot of talk, and a lot of writing. Getting to know each other in a deeper way, bit by bit, layer by layer.

This step feels simultaneously risky and risk-free. What have you got to lose? Only a deeply unsatisfactory status quo. Letting the heart shout out over the caution and judgments of the head is powerful stuff. It feels inordinately risky to those—like me—who have let their heads rule the roost for a long, long time. And yet, as soon as you have done it, and been honest with yourself, there is an immense sense of exhilaration. Just at having changed that one, deeply ingrained pattern. It gives you fuel and inspiration to address all the other challenges that then await.

FINDING YOUR MATCH—DO YOU KNOW WHAT YOU'RE LOOKING FOR?

One of the challenges with finding a match in the second half of life is simple scarcity. It is what one author refers to as a Thin Niche.[36] Online dating has hugely broadened the possibility of finding someone of an older age, but many people over age 30 struggle greatly with the entire concept, let alone its implementation. Although fully a third of American marriages between 2005 and 2012 were initiated online, many of the people I interviewed found it a harrowing and depressing experience.

One of the problems, especially for women, is that there is simply too much choice. As noted by Sheena Iyengar in *The Art of Choosing*, too much choice shuts people down, pushing them to choose none of the overwhelming options on offer. She describes two supermarket experiments in which shoppers were offered a choice of different pots of jam. In the first version, they were given a choice of

---

36   Aziz Ansari and Eric Klinenberg, *Modern Romance: An Investigation*, Penguin, 2016

16 different flavours of jam. In the second, they were given a restricted choice of only four pots. Sales of jam were much stronger in the second staging than in the first.

I've long felt that what we need in almost every area of life are trusted filters. People or services who winnow down the overwhelming quantity of choice now on offer in almost every area of life— from jam to romance. If you are, like me, someone who would rather choose between three carefully curated, attractive options than search through thirty without any quality control, online dating poses a particular challenge. As though dating wasn't difficult enough at our advanced ages. If you add in overwhelming, un-curated choice, it gets worse.

So I've been dreaming of the ideal alternative. A dating service that would bring somewhat-selected singles over 50 together in small groups, preferably over a delicious dinner in an intimate home setting. You sign up to the service, and go to a dinner each month over the course of a year. And someone would actually meet each of these people first to ensure there aren't the scary sort of people that too many interviewees have complained of being introduced to online. A touch of personalization and heart, without too much of the dating agency type social engineering. And a lot more simply left to happenstance, one of those magic ingredients we've tried too hard to eject from our search for a soulmate. Of course, this already exists in a variety of places; one service in the US is aptly called Eight At Eight[37], eight single people for dinner at 8pm, although without being targeted at an older demographic.

One of the challenges many people find is that they have an unconscious and deeply frustrating tendency to repeat patterns from prior relationships that they would prefer to break. They choose the same sort of partner who causes the same sorts of triggers, creates the same kind of behaviours they want to overcome in a new relationship. As Mark Twain is attributed to have said, "History doesn't repeat itself, but it often rhymes." It is almost impossible to break a pattern unless you are acutely

---

37 See www.8at8.com

aware of what that pattern is. See it coming, know the triggers that make you routinely fall for it, and consciously resist falling for it – yet again. This is the technique that lies at the heart of cognitive behavioural therapy or CBT counselling.

An easy exercise to tease this out is to review the key relationships in your life to date. I call it the Three Pots of Jam analysis (see exercises at end of chapter). Doing this, with the three men I have had the most significant relationships with in my life (see prologue), I decided to agree with Kurt Vonnegut that "you're allowed to be in love three times in your life."[38]

As Mae West savvily concluded, "It's not the men in your life that matters, it's the life in your men." I discovered, doing this exercise, how much my current, late love resembles my first love. Almost as though I had immediately known the kind of profile I was after: creative, Renaissance-man type of polymath, tall and very charming. But in between, it was as though my biological programming took over and made me choose someone steadier, more dependable and more even-tempered. There is no doubt in my mind this was a wise choice of partner to parent children. He is a devoted father. There is also no doubt in my mind I find the others hopelessly seductive. They make me feel more of a woman, and a loveable one at that. Biology or psychology? In the end, the debate, while fascinating, doesn't change the way you feel. I wrote a short poem to Tim that expresses this:

---

38 Kurt Vonnegut, quoted in Maria Popova's newsletter *Brain Pickings,*
     https://www.brainpickings.org/2012/11/15/kurt-vonnegut-love/

Balance
Avivah Wittenberg Cox

You

Not only

Make my heart swell and

My body purr.

You also (best of all)

Make my brain bounce. And that!

That's the key that

Unlocks

All the rest.

· ·

THE TOOLKIT

· ·

FINDING YOURSELF

There are a huge numbers of different personality tests available today. It's not necessary to do many, but they are useful in establishing a relatively objective picture of how you see yourself, compared to the results of many millions of others. They are also very interesting to use as a discussion basis with any potential partner, as the differences that arise between you will become quite visible, and you will have tools to name and explain them. Once you've done two or three of them, the messages you discover about yourself are usually coming across loud and clear. It may not be news, but it's helpful to clarify and confirm.

HELEN FISHER (MATCH.COM) 4 TYPES[39]

Are you explorer, builder, director or negotiator? Helen Fisher is the science behind online dating website empire Match.com. She has developed a test that identifies your two top drivers, and suggests how successfully different pairs of types fit. I'm an explorer-negotiator, and Tim is a director-explorer. It is true that the endless curiosity and desire to learn and grow that characterises our marriage is a key characteristic of the explorer type, of which Fisher herself is one. She says that explorers are more likely to switch partners, whereas builders will be the least

---

39 Helen Fisher, *Why Him? Why Her? How to Find and Keep Lasting Love,* Oneworld Publications, 2011

likely. This is the first time I've seen any research on the link between personality types and marital choices.

https://theanatomyoflove.com/relation-ship-quizzes/helen-fishers-love-test/

ENNEAGRAM

The Enneagram is a tool created in the 1950s, though based on earlier thinking, for describing nine different personality types. The interesting factor here is that each type has nine levels of evolution, each reflecting a progression towards a "best self." I have also found that the site's tool for checking compatibilities across types resonates quite powerfully with many. (Full disclosure: I'm type Seven and Tim is type Six.)

https://www.enneagraminstitute.com/guide-to-all-riso-hudson-tests/

ACROSS NATIONALITIES – GEERT HOFSTEDE TEST

These tests are used in global companies to help managers understand and work across different cultures. But I've found them very helpful at home, too, where the same challenges arise. If you are romantically involved with someone with a different cultural background, or even if you are yourself a mix of different cultural heritages, this test will help you discover whether you are a typical representative of the country you hail from, and how that compares to other nationalities. Fascinating and useful. You get your own score, and that of three countries that interest you.

https://catalog.feedbackdialog.com/a?k-w=generated1486535644661&rk=Ne427 75355355

FINDING OTHERS

Three Pots of Jam Analysis: What are the major relationships of your life? Feel free to add more, but focus on the most meaningful ones to you. Give each relationship a name that symbolizes the chapter of your life it occupies and the kind of couple you were (e.g. First Love, Journey through Hell, Summer of Life). Each partnership has its own particular dynamic. What was yours? What did you get from/ give to each? What did you learn about yourself from each of these experiences? Confucius advised to "study the past if you would define the future." This is a key exercise, so you may want to take a blank page and really spend some time analyzing each one. Do you see any patterns emerge? Are you repeating similar roles in similar sorts of relationships, or are they all very different? Before you leap into the next relationship, make sure you have digested and learned from your past ones, otherwise you are more likely to repeat unconscious patterns than to build a more satisfying love.

Are there any meaningful similarities or differences between them? What would you ideally like the next relationship to look like? What would you like to give to it and get from it? And remember, love always has something of hazard and happenstance. Leave yourself open to the unexpected.

MY THREE POTS OF JAM

RELATIONSHIP with (NAME)		RELATIONSHIP with (NAME)		RELATIONSHIP with (NAME)	
Symbolic LABEL		Symbolic LABEL		Symbolic LABEL	
What I Gave	What I Got	What I Gave	What I Got	What I Gave	What I Got
What I Learned		What I Learned		What I Learned	

COMPATIBILITY QUESTIONS

In 1997, four American psychologists devised a series of 36 questions[40] to test how quickly people could develop intimacy and interest in each other. When this was reproduced in January of 2015 in the *New York Times*, it received a huge response; they even created an app for it, see below.[41] Know someone you'd like to get to know better – much better—quickly? There are three sets of questions, 36 in all, which become increasingly personal. At the end of them, you are supposed to sit face to face, staring into each other's eyes silently for 4 minutes. It's fast, fun and quickly profound. But not for the weak of heart. If you find someone up to the test, that's already a pretty good sign!

---

40   Raymond Aron et al, "The Experimental Generation of Inter-Personal Closeness," *Personality and Social Psychology Journal,* 1997 http://journals.sagepub.com/doi/pdf/10.1177/0146167297234003

41   Mandy Len Catron, "To Fall In Love With Anyone Do This," *The New York Times,* December 2015 http://www.nytimes.com/2015/01/11/fashion/modern-love-to-fall-in-love-with-anyone-do-this.html

SET 1: SAMPLE QUESTIONS	SET 2: SAMPLE QUESTIONS	SET 3: SAMPLE QUESTIONS
1. Given the choice of anyone in the world, whom would you want as a dinner guest? 2. Would you like to be famous? In what way? 3. Before making a telephone call, do you ever rehearse what you are going to say? Why? …	1. If a crystal ball could tell you the truth about yourself, your life, the future or anything else, what would you want to know? 2. Is there something that you've dreamed of doing for a long time? Why haven't you done it? 3. What is the greatest accomplishment of your life	1. Make three true "we" statements each. For instance, "We are both in this room feeling … " 2. Complete this sentence: "I wish I had someone with whom I could share … " 3. If you were going to become a close friend with your partner, please share what would be important for him or her to know.
After all the questions have been mutually answered by both partners, spend four minutes looking silently into each other's eyes.		

RELATED APP

36 Questions to Fall in Love With, Krister Johnson: Lists the questions in easy-to-read format, and shares them out between two people. It even has a timer for the 4-minute, silent-stare-in-to-each-others'-eyes exercise at the end. Available on the App store.

BOOKS

Vincent Deary, *How to Live, Tome 1: How We Are,* Penguin, 2014

One of my favourite books. It's all about the challenge of change, and the internal process of adaptation and transformation that follows. He draws on his own life and struggles of leaving a calm job and marriage to go write a book in a cabin and figure himself out. A psychologist, he charts the journey of change through the moments of shock and disruption, then the incredible phase of fog and confusion, and the gradual re-emergence into an entirely new reality. He writes beautifully and even draws in very simple lines what it all looks like. Brilliant, wise and deep.

Alexandra Solomon, *Loving Bravely: Twenty Lessons of Self-discovery, 2017.*

A guide full of practical exercises to lead you through a complete self-review. Based on the highly reputed course Solomon, Marriage 101, Solomon teaches at Northwestern University.

Aziz Ansari and Eric Klinenberg, *Modern Romance: An Investigation, Penguin, 2016*

A comedian and a sociologist pair up to look at the modern perils and pleasures of online dating. Full of interesting and useful research, as well as a good guy's perspective on trying to find a soulmate. His bottom line on online dating? Give each person at least four tries … The laser-quick judgments we make of people on a first date when both are nervous and uncomfortable are neither fair nor accurate. Also, graduate quickly to face-to-face meetings; don't spend months on email before you meet in real space.

Laurie Davis, *Love @ First Click: The Ultimate Guide to Online Dating,* Atria Books, 2013

Since more than a third of marriages in the US now originate from online websites, it seems a shame not to learn how to use these tools well. For the older generation who may not want to hang out in bars or rely on friends, it's an unparalleled gateway to what it called a "thin niche:" the older crowd. It's also become increasingly diverse and segmented, so there are some sites that will be a better match for your style and preferences. Learning how to navigate the online world takes a bit of preparation. A good overall guide.

Susan Quilliam, *How to Choose a Partner,* Macmillan, 2016

A publication by the excellent UK School of Life, written by the UK's leading relationship expert, this is an easy-to-read deeper dive into this whole chapter. A step-by-step, very common-sense guide to sequencing and prioritising the search, not getting too obsessive about it all, and an invitation to give chance a chance.

Deborah Tannen, *You Just Don't Understand: Women and Men in Conversation,* Virago, 1992

This book on the different ways men and women communicate spent four years on the *New York Times* bestseller list, eight months at Number 1! That gives you an idea of how hungry people are to understand what's going on with their partners. It is essential reading for anyone who wants to be able to talk and be heard by someone of the opposite sex – especially if you live with them. There is a lot of misunderstanding that arises between two perfectly well-meaning people unwittingly anchored in cultural norms. I use all of Tannen's work in my gender-balancing work in organisations, and it's equally precious and necessary at home. So, in your next chapter, you may want to become what I call "gender bilingual," able to expertly navigate between the languages and expectations of both sides of the conversation.

VIDEOS

Hannah Fry, *"The Mathematics of Love"*

https://www.ted.com/talks/hannah_fry_the_mathematics_of_love

Fry reverse-engineers the online dating sites to be able to craft a profile that attracts the kind of men she is looking for. She is a mathematician, so this was easier for her than for most of us. But she found that her initial online search approach was all wrong and was delivering a series of uninteresting options. Once she figured it out, she met some very interesting men. And married one of them.

Sheena Iyengar, *"The Art of Choosing"*

http://www.ted.com/talks/sheena_iyengar_on_the_art_of_choosing?language=en

Iyengar is the economist responsible for the jam jar test described above. She proves that too much choice kills choice, which in a dating context means that focus and exploration may yield better results than multiplying options and dates. It's also a lot less tiring.

LOVING
Conscious (Re)Coupling

"Fatefully for our chances of happiness, in the Romantic ideology, love is understood to be an enthusiasm, rather than what it really is: a skill that needs to be learnt."

Alain de Botton

"You only live once, but if you do it right, once is enough."

Mae West

WHAT I LEARNED OF LOVE SO FAR

. . . .

I'VE LEARNED THAT LOVE either grows or dies. I've learned that the reality of love is steeped in the realities of power, independence and self-awareness. Love has changed because women, and some men, are demanding more of their relationships. Some partners are adapting to that request. Many are not.

I've learned that I've become deeply suspicious of the generalized assumption that a long marriage is better than two or three meaningful ones. A friend sent me a study carried out by Karl Pillemer from Cornell who has also written a book on *30 Lessons for Loving: Advice from the Wisest Americans on Love, Relationships, and Marriage.*[42]

We are all, I know, biased by our own life experiences, but Pillemer is seeking to prove his own situation, married for 36 years to his high school sweetheart. He is selling the idea that weathering it out leads to happiness in the end. Except, of course, that it doesn't feature those who redesigned their lives and found that yielded happiness, too. Nor does he refer to the fundamental shift in gender politics that underlies so much of the reality of what we call love.

---

42   http://www.usatoday.com/story/money/personalfinance/2015/01/06/retirees-love-marriage/20648553/

Very few books or commentators address this shift. Marriage has changed because women have changed. The power balance between men and women has changed profoundly. The combination of the Pill (which first appeared in 1960) and women's financial independence have created a situation where for the first time in history, women can choose who they love, who they stay with, or whether they decide to live on their own. For most of the couples in Pillemer's sample, average age 76, this simply wasn't a realistic option.

So his "research" doesn't really prove anything about what will work for couples who have such different life experiences, expectations and resources to actually execute on their preferences.

Helen Fisher, the Match.com scientist mentioned above, has a different take. She suggests that personality types affect marital outcomes and choices. In her typology of four, physiologically-based profiles (Explorer, Builder, Director, Negotiator), she suggests that the stable, conservative Builders are likeliest to stay together over the longest terms, while the variety-hungry Explorers will be more likely to wander into new waters. As an Explorer, I fit her theory.

So are we all just unconsciously moving along a predictable course? That colors the outcome. It's only when both men and women have something approaching a real choice that "happiness" research results become significant. Dan Gilbert, the author of *Stumbling on Happiness*, has proven just how good people are at explaining and rationalizing their own situations. So, he says, while all the happiness research proves that people are least happy when they have young children, most people will claim this is one of the happiest times of their lives. Staying with a spouse and learning to accept it because you have no option is a very different situation from what we see playing out just a generation later: an increase in people—mostly women—opting out because, for the first time in a few millennia of human history, they can. Comfortably. Maybe happily.

The myth of the ideal, lifelong relationship will not disappear quickly. It undeniably has advantages. I subscribed to it fully. How lovely to have the memories and children and dreams stay cohesively part of a single story. It's neat and tidy. So much less messy than having to deal with complex, recomposed families and multiple strings and relationships in so many directions. Yet like so many gender-related topics, our yearning for simplicity may not serve our need for growth and maturity. The world is complex, and consciously redesigning relationships that meet your maturing needs isn't, as so many would like to portray it, a capitulation to short-term selfish interests. It is what human life is all about: learning, growth and exploration with like-minded hearts and souls. Some people manage to do this while staying in the same relationship. If both partners are willing to explore and recreate their relationship based on evolving needs and aspirations, that sounds ideal. If one is simply settling into acceptance, and learns to come to terms with it, it is an entirely different choice, and one worth making clearly and consciously.

There is a concept of the "good enough" marriage. But as the explosion of relationship books suggest, the idea of "good enough" is not favoured by most humans. Michelle, who divorced her husband after his affair came to light, has a mantra she constantly re-examines:

Good, better, best

Never let us rest

Till good gets better

And better best

She urges, "Examine your life, and don't get lulled into the daily grind. It's a false sense of security. Pick up and create a better life. If you're given the privilege of a healthy body and mind, you owe it to yourself."

Skills, self-knowledge and education are just as useful in improving parent-child relationships as they are in solidifying marital relationships. It would be surprising as you watch conscious people get better at managing age, fitness and retirement, that they wouldn't also seek to build mastery at the key relationships in their lives.

Perhaps no one has expressed this better than the psychologist Erich Fromm in his famous *The Art of Loving*. He makes a persuasive case that you can become masterful at love, in the same way that you become masterful at anything: by making it your life's work. "The first step to take is to become aware that love is an art, just as living is an art; if we want to learn how to love we must proceed in the same way we have to proceed if we want to learn any other art, say music, painting, carpentry, or the art of medicine or engineering ... The process of learning an art can be divided conveniently into two parts: one, the mastery of the theory; the other, the mastery of the practice ... I shall become a master in this art only after a great deal of practice, until eventually the results of my theoretical knowledge and the results of my practice are blended into one – my intuition, the essence of the mastery of any art. But, aside from learning the theory and practice, there is a third factor necessary to becoming a master in any art – the mastery of the art must be a matter of ultimate concern; there must be nothing else in the world more important than the art. This holds true for music, for medicine, for carpentry – and for love. And, maybe, here lies the answer to the question of why people in our culture try so rarely to learn this art, in spite of their obvious failures: in spite of the deep-seated craving for love, almost everything else is considered to be more important than love: success, prestige, money, power – almost all our energy is used for the learning of how to achieve these aims, and almost none to learn the art of loving."[43]

One of the inspiring outcomes of the interviews I conducted with late love couples is how happy people become when they consciously re-design relationships in maturity. They make it the priority of their later lives. They draw lessons from the first half of life: about themselves, about relationships, about their purpose in life. And they learn to use this knowledge to carefully craft new alliances that they place at the very heart of their lives – and around which all the rest is consciously arranged.

David describes his late love as "profoundly safe. It is not what Elisabeth gives me, but what I give myself. I don't need her to complete me. It is an old cliché but true, we live in the moment. Every day,

---

43   Erich Fromm, *The Art of Loving*, 1956

we honour what each of us needs. We laugh, play, explore and travel together. Each of us is learning not to be a caretaker. We are not hiding. I have a new faith in myself, and that freedom that I feel, allows love to flow. Now, I just hope we live a long time…"

The care with which many of these couples intentionally design their lives together is fascinating to witness. They take time to really discuss and align on their bigger life goals, and then carefully put in place new systems and patterns to mutually reinforce each other.

Vincent Deary, in his best-selling book *How to Live*, describes how there is often a phase of deep discomfort that precedes change. People are stressed, uncomfortable or unhappy. A feeling that "something has to give" permeates life. Or change can be sudden and cataclysmic and blow in unannounced. In either case, there are years of turbulence that follow the arrival of change. This time is characterized by being thrown completely from all your habits and patterns, not knowing who or what to rely on. It usually means having to make new connections, new choices, and new moves. Once past, the dust settles on what might become a new phase, and people tend to "re-same." They recreate new patterns and habits so that large chunks of life can return to being unconsciously easy and effortless. This "re-saming" phase is very important for later life couples, and many seem to know it.

They are often aware the old habits are not welcoming to new loves and compromise and change will be required. It helps if this can be named, put on the table and agreed upon. It helps if people talk. Luckily, one of the great joys of older couples is they seem much more amenable to sharing, giving and taking in a less defensive way. They are wiser and less attached to things that earlier may have defined them. They are also more conscious of the preciousness of love, and often promote it to a higher place in their conscious priority ranking than it was in earlier and more striving decades.

Many of the men in late love couples recognize they are entirely different people than they were earlier in life. They have come to terms with their relative success—or lack of it—in life. They are not usually striving to prove anything, or to support families, or build identities. The testosterone levels that fuelled a variety of drives have fallen, making them calmer and more serene. Many of the men who had let the rational, analytical sides of their brains rule much of their lives and careers are more open to connecting their minds to their hearts. The wisdom of years is more receptive to the emotional realities of the world and its inhabitants.

Women in their later years, on the other hand, often seem to be increasingly energized with a sense of drive and purpose. They are, at least this current generation I am interviewing, (relatively) free of the earlier demands of life and families and particularly children. By their 50s, the kids are usually out of the house, if not out of their bank accounts. This creates a, sometimes surprising, sense of freedom and opportunity. Testosterone levels post-menopause rise, giving women an added energy and drive they may appreciate in careers and causes that begin to take off as they age. Because the traditional peak career age for men is younger, we don't expect or plan for women's career cycles[44]. For many ambitious women, the best career ages start post-40 and then keep rising. That means the 50s and 60s become women's best career decades, and since many of their partners are a bit older, and post-peak, this may even mean they have a retired, supportive partner at home for the first time.

Kathleen was married for 20 years to a man who was a 6-foot-6, charismatic leader in their community. He was a big personality whom she adored and supported. She had a small business as a financial planner, and many of the colleagues and acquaintances in his social network became her clients. He was very much the lead career, as well as the lead character in their couple. When he died, after a couple of years of shocked mourning, she entered a period of intense personal and professional growth. She created a new business, started to speak and run workshops nationwide and wrote an award-winning book. Her own late love, Charlie, is a retired engineer who loves to support her career. Financially and professionally successful in his own right, he now is thrilled to attend conferences where she speaks, or chauffeur her clients in and out from the airport. He is intensely proud of her,

---

44   Avivah Wittenberg-Cox, *Four Phases of Women's Careers: Becoming Gender Bilingual,* 20-first Publishing, 2016

and not in the slightest intimidated or jealous. He's done it, and enjoys giving himself fully and completely to playing supportive spouse. How many women have ever enjoyed such a thing?

This gender difference in career and life cycles is not often mentioned. In my work, I'm constantly working to build awareness of gender differences that impact business. But the gender differences are equally impactful at home. Most of the women interviewed played a lead role in raising children, which means their careers were affected in their 30s and 40s, while most of the men at this stage felt they were meant to provide financially for their families.

Robert admits that when his first daughter was born, he was an associate partner in an accountancy firm "clawing my way up the greasy career pole by putting in all the hours known to man." His wife, also a career woman, was left with the impossible tightrope of balancing her own work and a new baby, something she "did not find easy."

These roles can flip in later life, and women can take off and focus on careers while their partners can relax and enjoy their relative rest, and their wives' rise. Wouldn't it be interesting if this gender difference was celebrated and supported? What would it look like if we recognised that careers don't have to have the uniform, unbroken up-or-out trajectory of the 20th-century male? What if we acknowledged and facilitated women (and some men) benefiting from flexibility in their 30s, and women (and some men) accelerating careers in their 50s and 60s? Given women's relative longevity (women still outlive men on average by 6.7 years in the US and by 5.3 in the UK)[45], it may make sense for women's careers to peak relatively later. "Over a multi-stage life," write the authors of *The 100-Year Life*, "we expect that more households will be dual income and what will change will be the coordination between the two. This will enable switching between the two partners as each becomes the dominant earner at different stages."[46] They add that up to now, couples have focused a lot of

---

45 "Why is Life Expectancy Longer for Women than it is for Men?", *Scientific American*,
    https://www.scientificamerican.com/article/why-is-life-expectancy-lo/
46 Lynda Gratton and Andrew Scott, *The 100-Year Life: Living and Working in an Age of Longevity,* Bloomsbury, 2017

their personal/ professional juggling over weeks or years. In the future, they will be planning and coordinating their respective roles over decades.

We lose the complementarity of our differences when we try to all behave the same—at home or at work. The reality is couples that celebrate and embrace their differences—and use them across all areas of their lives—may be better off.

One of the great joys of my current couple resides in these differences. Tim is good at so many things I'm bad at. He follows through, where I stop after having sketched out the big picture. He loves tools and plumbing and knows everything about real stuff like houses and rot and electricity. I can change a light bulb, but I'd rather design a website or sit by a window to write a book. He had a big corporate job early on, now he's a sculptor. I was a laid-back freelancer early on, now I'm a globe-trotting consultant. I've always wanted a dog; he's ready to walk her when I'm not home. I love to cook, he loves to eat. In almost every way, our energies are different and complementary. The sum of the two makes for a deliciously balanced life.

Very early in my career, I did a series of in-depth interviews of dual career couples where the wife was an alumnae of the international business school I attended in France, called INSEAD. At the time, I was trying to figure out how to best manage my own couple's career options. As became quickly clear to me from the interviews the happiest and most at ease couples were those who had very different and complementary career tracks. One would have a corporate career, the other would have an academic or entrepreneurial path. One couple, both Harvard Business School alumni, was quite explicit: the consultant husband would bring in the short-term, keep-the-family-afloat income, while the wife left her corporate job to have children and start an entrepreneurial business in the kitchen, aiming for long-term pay off. It worked. He eventually left his job to join her company, which they later sold and underwrote a comfortable later life of volunteering and angel investing. But they leveraged different skills, interests and especially time lines to consciously craft a family life, and a family career. Very few couples work together to craft optimal family planning around both personal and professional dimensions. There is still a push towards equality—both should enjoy the same careers at the same times. This is much harder to pull off.

This may be challenging in younger generations as they increasingly leave behind traditional gender roles. I was brought up in this mold. I could do anything and everything any man could do. While we may want to get rid of the stereotypes and the automatic defaults (she cooks, he takes out the garbage), we still want to explore and celebrate the differences. As I age, I love that Tim does many of the stereotypically "manly" things I admit to having no interest in. He loves machines. I love not worrying about them. I love being able to concentrate on my career, knowing the kids have flown, and the home front is under control. It is the first time in my life I can luxuriate in a relatively one-track mind. I remember my friend Andrea after leaving her senior executive husband saying she would never have another relationship with a man in a suit. She had her sights set on someone with a tool belt around his jeans. Really what she was yearning for was the gender differences we have been too focused on erasing.

Too many egalitarian marriages are hurt by the same insistence on similarity (or conformity) that I've seen hurt gender balance in companies. When men and women are the same, there is less appreciation for what the other brings to your life. If both can do and be everything the other can, the "otherness" that brings so much excitement and mystery and attraction to relationships disappears behind a fog falsely called equality. This is what psychologist Esther Perel laments in her book *Mating in Captivity*[47] about the failing libidos of modern couples. "Partners today," she writes, "need to negotiate their dual needs for familiarity and novelty, their wish for certainty and surprise."[48]

This is a million miles on from Simone de Beauvoir's historic affirmation that "one is not born, but rather becomes, a woman." The time and the context of mid-20th-century post-war society called

---

47   Esther Perel, *Mating in Captivity, Reconciling the Erotic and the Domestic,* Hodder & Stoughton, 2007
48   Esther Perel, "The Double Flame Reconciling Intimacy and Sexuality, Reviving Desire," from *Treating Sexual Desire Disorders: A Clinical Casebook,* The Guilford Press, 2010

for a drive towards equality. Women became the second sex by the prejudices of a society that would not let them blossom and limited their access to education and autonomy. Now that women are the majority of the world's educated graduates, and too many men and boys are challenged and failing to adapt, [49] it may be time to revisit and re-evaluate our understandable aversion to gender differences. They have been used for millennia to hold us down. But in the world that is coming, where brains have replaced brawn at every turn, and smart, win/win collaboration is becoming more valued than blind, win/ lose competition, differences are increasingly seen as a source of enrichment.

MIT did a series of studies of a variety of teams where some teams were dominated by men, others by women, and some were a balance of both. They found the smartest teams were balanced, and the team with more women did better than the teams with none.[50] When universities as prestigious as MIT start publishing data like this, and when companies start working hard to gender-balance their organizations to tap into the value of these differences, when Google can chart the different usage patterns of the web by men and women, it seems interesting that people should be so allergic to acknowledging that differences exist. And while I understand the fear, I regret the loss. Complementarities in styles and approach are proven at work. Do we really need to prove them at home?

Cultivating and recognizing each other's differing interests and strengths may become much more natural as the genders rebalance. Today's young people pride themselves on being gender neutral, or even post-gender. However, most feminists are born when they have children. Traditional gender roles are hardest to resist when children enter the equation. The most progressive men start to falter when their own career prospects are called into question. This won't change until parenting is a much more gender-balanced occupation. As millennials hit their parenting strides, the harsh reality of who

49 "The Weaker Sex," *The Economist,* May 30, 2015
50 Anita Woolley, Thomas W. Malone, Christopher F. Chabris, "Why Some Teams Are Smarter Than Others," *New York Times,* January 16, 2015 *http://www.nytimes.com/2015/01/18/opinion/sunday/why-some-teams-are-smarter-than-others.html*

will babysit has not evolved, and younger fathers find themselves forced to make choices they once decried. [51] I am a bit dubious about any single generational cohort's ability to dramatically shift the power balance. The public policy and systems that create the imbalances will have to adapt first. Hopefully, over time, both men and women will gain more flexibility not only in what they do each day, but also how they manage their roles over their lifetimes. Our late love couples, who don't much care anymore about societal roles, are an interesting laboratory for some of these trends.

Before our wedding, the differences in my own late love couple became increasingly clear. I love to effortlessly blue sky plan, and then wing it. Tim, a former event and exhibition organizer, likes everything timed, planned and documented in the most excruciating detail. A kindly coach friend, Lesley, watching us try and negotiate our way through, took pity and had us do a decision-making-style test. It confirmed what we already knew, that we were very different, that I tended to the red-orange side of the analysis, which means that I am an easy entrepreneur, with a multitude of ideas that explode like popcorn. Tim is more blue-green, which reflects the more rational and data-driven side of the brain. Under stress, people have a tendency of moving towards a more extreme version of their preference. So we became ever more pronouncedly different. It's good to know. And helps to be able to put a name on a behavior. However, as Lesley explained, a majority of men fall into the blue/green spectrum, and it's characteristic of blue/green profiles to be annoyingly convinced they are right (though I'm not immune to this failing either!). These kinds of tools are helpful in predicting behavioural tendencies, being able to recognise them when they arise and navigate through them. There is a certain distancing in these personality analyses that helps both partners not make the differences quite so personal.

The "blending" of the sexes described above is more common in Anglo-Saxon countries (US, UK, Australia), than it is in more Latin cultures. I lived for almost 30 years in Paris, and found that Frenchwomen (and men) had an intriguingly different approach to gender differences. I worked

---

51   Clair Cain Miller, "Millennial Men Find Work And Family Hard To Balance," *New York Times,* July 2015
     http://www.nytimes.com/2015/07/31/upshot/millennial-men-find-work-and-family-hard-to-balance.html?abt=0002&abg=1

with a lot of highly educated career women over the years. Many Frenchwomen, I noticed, never lost their femininity in their rise to power. They used their differences, were proud of them, and seemed generally less antagonistic and resentful towards men. They enjoyed flirting and seduction in ways that I initially found reprehensible, until I found it soul-saving. It was in France that I learned to become "gender bilingual," combining masculine and feminine attributes, styles and even dress in very conscious combinations. In Anglo-Saxon countries, the push for equality seems to have led far more to women adopting male behaviors and styles in order to succeed. Women pay for that at work, as I don't think this strategy has paid off particularly well. We also pay for it at home. Couples trying to occupy and defend similar spaces often seem lost in a competitive struggle for identical identities.

As I listen to these late love couples establish themselves as long-term committed pairs, complementarity and recognition of differences seems to be the name of the game.

THE TRUTH ABOUT POWER

I've always thought the reality of most couples can be analyzed in terms of their relative power balance. This may not be the most romantic view of supposedly amorous unions, but it is a key criterion in this transitional moment in gender history and in the longevity stakes. There are so many unspoken realities in the intimate lives of two people, and traditions play a huge part in the power story.

Power relations can tell us so much about a couple's health, though how it looks on the outside isn't necessarily the same as how it feels from the inside. As Ethel Person writes in her book, *Feeling Strong*, "However intricate, varied and surprising lovers' arrangements to achieve a balance of power may be, the only criteria for judging them is whether the lovers feel satisfied that neither is being unduly exploited ... When love is on the wane, power manifests itself in a tug-of-war ... when the expectations of passionate love are unfulfilled, the wish to give and sacrifice for the beloved deteriorates into disappointment, self-justification, resentment and a desire to receive. Mutuality is then replaced by a struggle for priority. An embattled love may no longer be committed to the couple but may instead decide to provide for himself."[52]

One of my oldest friends watches in apoplectic resentment as her 70-year-old mother services her father's every need. Her grandmother, she says, was even worse, and never sat down at the table, but was always busy serving everyone else's needs. From her generational standpoint, these patterns are inadmissible and she struggles to eradicate their weight on her own conscience. But she is also forced to admit that both her parents appear entirely content with their arrangement. She's the only one who has an issue with it.

But that was then. A combination of changes hits the generation of couples now in their 50s and affects what may, until then, have been an acceptable balance of power. In a single decade, many men's careers begin to slow or come to an end, many women's work and financial clout may be simultaneously growing, and the pull of caring for children suddenly disappears. For many couples, this is a dramatic redrawing of the power lines. The emotions around each of these transitions can be very different. Women are generally thrilled and energized by the sudden freedom of late careers—something that may have eluded them earlier on. Some men are dubious about the end of their professional identities and earning power, while others delight in being able to relax at last.

The reality is that this phase is not a single phase. It is three different phases, each with huge emotional power, all thrown together in a single family with enormous connected interference. Children leaving home, careers taking off and/or careers coming to an end are three very different journeys. They do not all make for complementary companions. The ability to plan and manage this phase, and to ensure that these parallel journeys can be experienced as mutually satisfying and enriching, would help minimise the unhelpful impression that power balances are flipping upside down.

---

52 Ethel Person, *Feeling Strong: How Power Issues Affect Our Ability to Direct our Own Lives,* HarperCollins, 2002

So for example, in your couple:

- Who makes key decisions?
- Whose job takes the lead?
- Who makes (or brings) most of the money?
- Who talks more at dinner parties?
- Who initiates sex?
- How do arguments get resolved?

These are all interesting measures underlining how two individuals experience their relationship.

Among my interviews for this book, the happiest relationships tended to be more egalitarian, each partner comfortable with the natural give and take of influence, compromise and support. The emerging reality of more power-balanced (and usually fairly powerful) couples has been called the "personal growth marriage" by Northwestern University psychologist Eli Finkel. These are marriages where both partners are ambitious about self-fulfilment, and see their relationship as an essential part of self-growth. "Partners in these mini-power couples are attuned to each other's aspirations. Fundamentally, they are there to help each other grow."[53] When executed well, personal growth marriages are as good as it gets. "The best marriages today are almost certainly better than the best marriages the world has ever seen."[54] The gap between these excellent relationships and the rest, however, is growing apace. And the challenge is that these relationships take time and effort and focused intention. They also take skill. And they are more likely to occur in carefully crafted, late love couples.

Adam Grant, in his book *Give and Take*, talks about preferences in inter-personal relationships. He categorizes people as takers, givers or matchers. Takers default to maximizing whatever they can

53 Zosia Bielski, "Are We in the Golden Age of Marriage?", *Globe and Mail,* July 2, 2015
     http://www.theglobeandmail.com/life/relationships/are-we-in-the-golden-marital-age/article25224753/
54 Eli Finkel, "Current Directions in Psychological Science"

get in a given interaction, while givers tend to try to be of service. Matchers adopt a fairness approach of "tit for tat." He suggests, contrary to what many might think, the "giver" is the better strategy and one that works better than most people think in the work world. He then goes on to make the general assumption that in our personal lives, we default more readily to be givers where "we contribute whenever we can without keeping score."

I wish. Many marriages bear more resemblance to the work world than many of us think. If one partner feels entitled to "taking" and the other has been raised or socialised to be a "giver," then you get the kind of marriage that many "givers" want to leave. Many of the people I interviewed who left marriages found they were married to "takers." I'd argue that what most of the women I talked to wanted at home, above anything, was a matcher. You don't actually want someone selflessly giving all the time without being able to take. Healthy selfishness is a wonderful thing in great couples. You have a partner willing to help you get what you want or need, and vice versa. There is nothing more delightful.

Too many people have been educated never to ask for some of their most profound yearnings. Some spend a lifetime believing they don't deserve it. Most of the women I interviewed felt there was a power imbalance in their early relationships. This ranged from being expected to serve (socially, sexually and/or domestically), to feeling unsupported as their own external power began to increase.

Andrea met her husband-to-be during her bar exams. They both started their careers with the same employer and similar jobs, but he quickly pulled ahead as they started having children. Nonetheless, they were both highly educated, well-paid professionals with a comfortable urban lifestyle. With the birth of her third child, Andrea decided to stop working for a while to take care of the family. The same week her pay check stopped, her husband of seven years transformed unrecognisably - almost overnight. He announced he was giving her a weekly budget and became increasingly controlling of her every purchase. His need for control combined with her need for peace-making. She knew the role well as the eldest child of an alcoholic father. She had spent her childhood trying to make peace between her parents. Now she found herself in a repeat production, with relatively little negotiating power—she had young children, no salary and a quickly diminishing sense of self-esteem. She stuck it out for another decade...

When she met her own late love, her life was transformed. She discovered the pleasure of a balanced relationship for the first time, with someone who wanted to give as well as take. In her own words:

I left with absolutely nothing, and the very first day in my new home, I started bawling. A couple of friends dropped in and saw me through. I can do this, I learned. I was very proud of my courage. The very first night I went to bed alone in my new home, I started feeling hope. It was already so much better than where I had been. At the very least, I was in control of my life. And there was the possibility of new love.

My ex accused me of being incapable of affection. I learned, a very pleasant surprise, that I could be loving and affectionate. It's never lost, it's always there, just waiting. A whole world opens up, there is so much happiness ahead. I'm even dreaming again! I look forward to growing old together, and all the things we can do together. I marvel at the optimism that has arrived, just by choosing hope.

We don't name the dynamics of power in relationships. We want to pretend we are equal, or power doesn't matter, or we won't wield it for or against each other. None of that seems to be true. Power is a central issue to the current rebalancing that is going on between men and women. The rise of women is overturning the classic balance in many homes, one that some men welcome, others resist. Men's attitude to this shift is a crucial determinant in the success of couples. But just as there is both conscious and unconscious bias between genders at work, there may be even more at home. How ready are both men and women in relationships to accept and adore partners who behave outside of conventional gender roles? Will men love and support increasingly more powerful/accomplished/higher-earning wives? And will wives be able to love and admire less powerful/accomplished/lower-earning husbands?

I was having dinner with five girlfriends shortly after my own separation several years ago. They were all successful women in a variety of fields. As I shared my news with them, we began a conversation about how comfortable our husbands were with our success. What struck me that evening was that half the group said their husbands were their biggest supporters, cheerleaders and reciprocal mentors. The other half said their husbands weren't comfortable with their growing reputations, and hated being dragged along to their own business events. They hated being called Mr. (Wife's Surname).

This is hard and unexplored territory. How many men are truly comfortable with (relatively—it's always entirely relative) successful and powerful wives? It still takes quite a rugged sense of self-esteem to weather the societal pressures and judgments that can result. While it has been said that behind every successful man there is a great woman, the reverse is less discussed. Aside from the occasional exception like Sheryl Sandberg's very public acknowledgement of her extraordinarily supportive spouse (tragically lost too young), the reality is that most powerful women have equally powerful husbands. Otherwise the reversal of roles too often breeds intimidation or resentment.

Intimidation is an issue that too many successful women discover has poisoned their marriages. They married men who were proud of their brains and skills. Many of these men would vehemently deny the issue, and insist they really are their wives' most ardent cheerleaders. But consciously or not, many men are not yet at ease with women who shine a bit too brightly. This is also true at work, of course, but it is far more wounding when it happens at home, with the person you were led to believe would be your prime cheerleader.

Aileen suffered from this problem. "I left school at 16 and became a secretary, then a community worker where I managed a lot of projects. I eventually trained as a counsellor and got my Masters in psychotherapy. My ex was envious while seeming supportive. He only ever worked for two companies. He liked that I made the changes, and then punished me for it." Aileen's therapy allowed her to see the patterns that had developed in her life and to challenge whether they were true. This gave her the confidence to walk away from her marriage.

Similarly, of the group I had dinner with, all the women who described their spouse's reluctance to celebrate their successes ended up divorced. The couples with enthusiastic partners continue to enjoy the rewards of mutual self-enhancement and growth.

In later love, couples can more easily correct for past imbalances. Many of the women I interviewed are at the peak of their professional lives in their 50s and 60s, while many of their later partners will be past it – or comfortably ensconced in "wise elder" roles. This creates an ideal opportunity for knowledgeable, supportive men supporting women with expanding dreams of impact and influence. It's like the flip side of what so many women experienced in their 30s, when so many slowed down to support children and let their husband's careers take the lead. For both partners, it can be a heady time exploring the pleasures of giving and taking in entirely new ways.

RITUALS OF ROMANCE

I'm a big believer in daily rituals. As we learn more about reprogramming the brain, it comes as no surprise that the rituals and repetitions of love will have an impact on the relationship it holds. Once you know that the act of smiling can improve your mood, or read the research on how meditation can re-program neural pathways, then the intentional re-design of couple's rituals becomes increasingly important. It is a good moment to think carefully about the basic architecture of the life you want to create together. Will there be some things you hold to and want to re-program into your shared life?

I had several.

BREAKFAST—PAUSING BEFORE YOU LEAP

Tim used to wake each morning to the BBC's Radio 4 news as his alarm. He'd go to bed well past midnight, sleep a small handful of hours to as late as he could afford, then dash out the door after downing a cup of coffee and some cold cereal. I've spent the last few years reading about the impacts of sleep, priming, and meditation on happiness. I can't imagine a worse way of waking then to be immediately assaulted with the media's ritual litany of global catastrophes, repeated in 10-minute loops.

Rushing into action, whether it is daily or in times of crisis, is not usually very effective. In *The Pause Principle*, Kevin Cashman says that too many CEOs want to dash into action before stepping back to look at the bigger picture. "We don't need to do more; we need to pause more."[55] My man was a pure product of this "doing" culture. The older I get, the more attached I am to starting my days calmly and serenely. My recent rule is to do what I care most about first thing in the day. Since this is often newer, more creative work, I used to leave it to fill small corners of time that might end up being free in the agenda. Now, I start with it, so I know I will get it done, no matter what shows up to disrupt the day. The same is true for breakfast. If our priority is the couple we create, it should come first—in the day, in every way. So that's where we start. With time, and each other. Across a very small table in a cozy kitchen.

Tim and I have intentionally decided to wake to each other first. To turn and smile and hug and be grateful for the human being we have chosen to share our life with. To take a little bit of time every morning (almost) to express love and gratitude and appreciation. It doesn't take a decade of neuroscience research to convince you that mirroring neurones and stimulating hormones and lighting the pleasure nodes of your brain is going to give you a better start to your day than an urgent update on the latest catastrophe from the far side of the planet.

---

55   Kevin Cashman, *The Pause Principle: Step Back to Lean Forward,* Berrett-Koehler Publishers, 2012

Instead, we sit down together to breakfast, my favorite meal of the day. To carefully brewed coffee, and toast and a sharing of the day to come. Time is ours to design, and claiming a half hour, before the day leaps into high gear, shores both of us up—with energy and spoken commitments and supportive nudging of each other's goals and projects. Better than any pill, a hug of belief.

The magic of touch is something so many couples talked about, usually with glee at the sudden discovery of its astonishing power. Andrea talks about the wonderful, reciprocal priming of a loving touch. "I love to start the day, and end the day," she says, "in a kind of happy bookends, with human, physical touch. It is so important to my well-being. Before, I cringed at touch. Same act, now with entirely different feelings."

I love this idea of the importance of bookends, at the beginning and end of days. So while every day begins with breakfast, the end of the day is also a short, conscious ritual of gratitude.

THE MILK JUG

There is a small white milk jug in my man's kitchen. Its defining characteristic is its simplicity – in both colour and form. And its source, of course. It comes from my man's mother, and reminds him of her.

I never, sadly, met her. I came along decades after she died, too young. Yet I feel a strange connection to this woman. I share her son with her. And I have inherited, gratefully, her legacy: the way this man loves women. I know that he has learned to hold me, caress me, lavish love upon me, from her. The way he lovingly cradles my face and gazes deeply, deeply into my eyes, has a primeval echo. An innate naturalness about it, as though he had learned to love as he learned to breathe.

She must have adored this boy, her youngest son, her familial soulmate. Listened to him, nurtured his sensitivities, nourished him with ideas, daily homemade desserts, and a teacher's faith in education and ideals. Their closeness I measure in the openness of his heart, my ability to worm into the very depths. My hand in his echoes the trust he had in hers. Ah, mothers!

Even her frustrations have been fertile soil. The workaholic husband, over-brimming with busyness, has been a cautionary role model. My man knew that his mother would have liked more. More attention, more time. He has been, at times, frustrated with his father for not giving his mother more of what she yearned for. So he has, imprinted within him, an understanding of the cost of his own inherited preference for over-filling time with tasks.

I love breakfast. Love the notion of pausing before running. Of the mindful meeting of coffee and toast. Carefully spread with salted butter, the kind with chunks of salt from the ocean. A reminder of the bigger outer forces we will soon be composing with. Where he had long adopted the modern habit of a snack on the run, or coffee at his desk, I carefully set the table each morning, and sit, willing us to begin each day as we end it, talking, together. The bachelor's default, the radio waking him to the catastrophic news of the day, yielded to a daily choice of musical accompaniment for the slosh of milk he pours from his mother's pitcher. His cup runneth over.

I have now moved into my man's home. He has wanted to make it ours, not his. So we have painted, and renovated and shifted things around. Colour has melted over minimalism. The kitchen is now lime green, the fridge is full of food. A new pantry is brimming with cookbooks and grains and spices. The dining room pulses with people from his past and mine, intertwining our futures with our pasts.

Last year, I offered him a milk frother. A sleek aluminium design, it heats milk up into a bubbly magic. It isn't meant to replace the milk jug, but is a respectful nod to its genitor. She poured on the white purity of first love. I have warmed life up and filled it with light and joyful bubbles. She was his first love. I will be his last. Together, in man and milk.

THREE THINGS

It's one of those mindfulness exercises I picked up along the way, and I find it is a wonderful talisman into sleep. We each take turns describing the three things we are most grateful for that day. It sounds silly and a bit artificial, but I find it endlessly fascinating to hear how another human being experienced our shared history, slice by slice. We are sometimes struck by the same things, sometimes very different. Sometimes things are huge and deep (my son's toast at our wedding), sometimes light and almost invisible (the sight of a bat against a starlit summer night).

And as an antidote to the evening news that puts our daily attention on everything that is wrong with the world, this simple ritual reminds us of the beauty and grace we are gifted every single day.

I can think of no better way to ease into dreamland. Usually, we humans are rushing through so many different things and events and information in any given 24 hours that we don't even have the time to remember what happened, let alone digest it. At our advancing age, where short-term memory begins to flag, taking a moment to think back to what happened during the day, what struck you and what you want to celebrate and share, feels a bit like imprinting. You grab the best images as they flit by and try to pull them into your consciousness for safe-keeping. Naming them and describing them pulls them from oblivion. Sharing them enriches your partnership with joy, doubling it as you relive it in the telling.

Andrea and Mark walk every evening after dinner, rain or snow. They explore the city streets in which they live and discuss their day while digesting their dinner. They are both fairly athletic, and they love to move and get air. This is a way of combining ritual with a natural, shared preference. As simple as that. For Elisabeth and David, it is a very particular kind of tea, served in carefully selected cups, in Elisabeth's wingback chairs. Michelle has this advice for end-of-day debriefs: "Marriage is something you will into being every day. Stop. Breathe. Think. Ask. Choose your fights. When you get into discussion, be careful what you say. There is no scoring points. Keep it civil all the time. Make an effort. Talk about things."

How and where do you debrief your days and your thoughts? Do you make the time, or like many, drop exhausted into bed for a few minutes of sleepy pillow talk before one of you nods off.

WHAT DOGS TEACH US ABOUT LOVE

For most late love couples, children are part of the baggage they bring, not a project they undertake together. But adopting a dog was about as close as I can imagine to revisiting parenthood.

I have wanted a dog all my life. My eldest brother was allergic to them and so was my ex-husband. So I spent 50 years yearning for a four-legged friend. My daughter yearned right along with me. When Tim and I seriously considered offering her a dog for her last year at home, she was ecstatic. It was certainly one of the things that made our home feel attractive and welcoming to her—the presence of the most adorable little miniature spaniel. She named her Princess Daisy. I knew the dog would have a huge and healing impact on my daughter. What I hadn't at all expected was her impact on Tim and me, both individually and as a couple.

It is hard to explain how big something so small can be. Daisy is a tiny thing, some 7 kilos of mostly eyes, ears and love. Tim was more of a cat man, and a bit dubious at this sudden incursion in his up-to-now bachelor life. Daisy was his first introduction to something as entirely dependent on him as a child. And like so many parents, he awakened to the role. In an echo of how he had awakened to my loving him, he was daily invited to respond to the outpouring of affection and attention from this four-legged, fast-track education to loving and being loved. The difference (okay, I know there are a few more) was that I could—and can—survive without him. But once my daughter went off to college and I was travelling for work, Daisy was completely and utterly dependent on him and only him. He often says this is the biggest change in his life. From a lifetime of independence to having to think about meals and walks and balls is a metaphor for what love brings into life. It isn't all passion and soul-matedness and discussing great books and movies in the private haven of the garden, although all of that is there. It is also the repetitive task of caring for loved ones, and translating that love into commitment, continuity and daily life. And to consciously invest these small acts with big ideas. Daisy has gifted Tim with dependence, and he has responded with a rather astonishing level of adoration spurred by responsibility. The two of them now are a picture of accomplished, mutual partnership.

For me, Daisy has become—quite seriously—a role model. It is hard to find an earthly creature so well designed to give and receive love. This seems a legitimate purpose for later life. In becoming so well loved, I have become much more open to receiving love—from everyone. Which suddenly meant I attracted it more than I used to, just as Daisy does from almost everyone she approaches with her eager tail wagging and her expectation of being adored. I have also become far more generous in loving others. More giving, more appreciative, and less attached to other's skills (or lack thereof) of loving in return. This remains a work in progress, but Daisy embodies in my daily life an aspirational example of what comes from loving naturally, without constraint or calculation.

For us as a couple, Daisy has become an entity that somehow turns us into something more than a couple. More of a family. She rounds us out, we worry about her together, take care of her together, walk her together. She functions as a child, without the complications. She is glue and joy, and cuddles up between us in the morning as delightedly as any two-year-old greeting a new day with unabashed delight. She dashes to greet us as we return home, investing the notion of home with the celebratory excitement of returns and completion. She is happiest when we are together, and sometimes refuses to play ball if there is only one of us there to throw it. She seems to somehow mirror the love we feel for each other, and as she basks in its warmth and looks so happy and whole, we warm to the reflection of love's rays.

SHARING PASSIONS

Many of the individuals who fall into later love have earlier passions they continue, a variety of hobbies, causes or communities they are attached to. Once you get together, there is often some negotiation about whether these will be shared or will be pursued independently. For us, I had a strong attachment to a tiny, faraway institute in the northwestern corner of New York State called Chautauqua (CHQ.org), where there is an annual summer festival of talks and culture. My kids have spent two weeks a year of most of their lives in this village. My mother, who lives relatively close by in Toronto, visits every summer. It is about as close to roots as my two European-born kids will ever have. I love it for its unusual bringing together of so many of my disparate interests—music of all kinds, lectures, theatre, dance, and a community that revels in the mix. It's a 150-year-old utopia of lifelong learning and engagement in the world's big themes all from the haven of a no-car Victorian village on the shores of a very small, northern American lake.

It is also very American. This is not every Brit's cup of tea. Would Tim, so grounded in London, be willing to suddenly transplant to a country neither of us was from, and become part of a community of Americans? Would I be willing to give him the choice? My kids, especially my son, were particularly attached to it. It was the most stable, unchanging piece of their international lives. I had modelled this summer home on the family homes I had seen while living in France. So many French families were knitted together by a home (usually old, a bit run down and in some gorgeous, rural part of the country). They would routinely get together for holidays and vacations in these places. Generations would mix and pass on their stories and traditions. As the citizen of a new-world country with little history and the descendant of a family tree decimated by war, I lusted after the invisible glue of roots. Chautauquans love roots. It's a place full of multi-generational families, traditions and history. It boasts the oldest book club in the US and the first women's club. Chautauqua shares my own yearning for roots and rituals. Like me, it's a bit of a misfit. It sits as an exception in a big country driven by very different values.

For so many of the couples I interviewed in Chautauqua, the place itself was one of the test criteria for their new unions. One half was deeply invested in the place, and the other was usually only fully accepted once they had displayed a similar level of adoration. It's not a sect, but it does elicit similar levels of commitment. "He had to pass the Chautauqua test first, of course," laughed Martha. "I'd never be able to give up my summers here." She brought him to Chautauqua for the weekend, then bought him a gate pass for the following summer. "He freaked out," she remembers, laughing. Now, he's as hooked as she is. "When you marry the first time," he says, "you build a dream. Second time, you live the dream."

Luckily, Tim totally subscribed to the vision of Chautauqua, the menu of options and the community. He had a lot more trouble adopting the concept of summer.

A few years before I fell in love with Tim, I fell in love with a model of working encountered in Chautauqua. Neighbours across the street from the place we rented owned their home and worked from there throughout the summer. They both travelled a lot, and would simply fly to Japan or California, as needed. They were another light bulb in my life. If they could do it, so probably could I. I bought a house in Chautauqua a couple of years later, borrowing to the hilt in a risky play on my future ability to pay up, and have since subscribed to the 10-2 model of work. Ten months in London and two months in Chautauqua.

For most of the year, I spend my time running around the globe and working at mostly one thing. For two months, I retreat to a small lakeside village, and allow myself time to write books, invent new projects, learn new things and meet new people and ideas. It's a mix of intellectual renewal and immense creative productivity. Not to mention food, family and community.

It took Tim several years to get used to the idea. In large part because, I must admit, while he has gamely shared my passions, I have been far less adept at sharing his. Tim is deeply in love with another woman he refers to as his mistress. This may not have helped ingratiate her in my heart.

She is a 7-meter steam boat called *Mischief,* and is rather more demanding than his wife. She takes weeks to prepare each spring, requires several people to get her into and out of the water, and her use depends on her passing her annual boiler inspections. She is a hymn to detail and planning and follow through. All my most distant characteristics. Tim will very happily spend days and weeks preparing her for a trip up the Thames. And I will happily join in on the trip. If it's sunny. And warm. The rest of that relationship is his own.

I suggest, in these matters, that much as it is important for Late Love couples to share passions, it is equally crucial that each person also have their own. Their own hobbies, their own spaces, their own time. (I hear some of you grumbling that this may seem self-serving at this point.) I love my yoga classes with a passion but have been unable to entice Tim into a downward dog. I regularly host Ladies Dinners to which he is firmly not invited, although he loves to squeeze in at the end for some left-over dessert and a sneak peek into the conversation. I take long walks with Daisy the dog along the river, and enjoy long stretches of daily alone time.

Finally, it's good for couples to find passions they can do together that are both new and shared. Tim and I have taken up dancing, and are learning Rock 'n' Roll with a charming Frenchman named Jean who gets a group of aging souls from the neighbourhood to shake their booty. It's silly and we are pretty hopeless, and regularly leave delighted in the energy that newness and effort bring.

A bit more seriously, we've also started to spend more time on conscious philanthropy and eldering – giving where we can in support of people and causes we believe in, and supporting the many young people who traipse through our home and lives. Tim read a book called *Doing Good Better,*[56] about donating to charities with the highest impact on the maximum number of people. This has caught both of our imaginations, and we have decided to spend a growing share of our time and resources on these efforts in the coming years.

---

56   Dr William MacAskill, *Doing Good Better: Effective Altruism and a Radical New Way to Make a Difference,* Guardian Faber, 2016

MONTHLY TALKS

So that's the fun, celebratory stuff. What about the stickier, more confrontational places that every human relationship encounters? For that, you may want to adopt a technique of "active listening." The fundamental dissonance that too many couples bump into, beautifully summarised by Terry Real, is that women don't feel heard and men don't feel appreciated. A way of addressing this is to ensure that both have a safe, regular place to communicate.

"An honorable human relationship … in which two people have the right to use the word 'love,'" wrote the poet Adrienne Rich, "is a process, delicate, violent, often terrifying to both persons involved, a process of refining the truths they can tell each other. It is important to do this because it breaks down human self-delusion and isolation. It is important to do this because in doing so we do justice to our own complexity. It is important to do this because we can count on so few people to go that hard way with us."[57]

Some couples, like David and Elisabeth, prefer to debrief misunderstandings right away, or day by day. I have learned to digest before debating. Also, while I'm a bit of a conflict avoidance type, I also know that what I say has often been experienced as more hurtful and cutting than I meant it to be. I have learned from life that my bark often has a much bigger impact than I think it does—or merits. One of my solutions is to write rather than talk. But that is hardly ideal in a couple.

Instead, Tim and I have regularly scheduled monthly talks. The rules of engagement are clear:

- **TALK:** Each partner, in turn, talks about their experience of the last month, including any issues, feelings, problems or requests that have come up. They get all the time they need to have it all out.

- **LISTEN:** The other partner listens intently, without speaking or reacting. Best even if there is no nodding, or other signal of agreement or disagreement. Look directly at your partner to show you are listening intently.

---

57   Adrienne Rich, *On Lies, Secrets and Silence: Selected Prose, 1966-1978,* W. W. Norton & Co, 1995

- **SUMMARIZE**: The listening partner then summarizes what they heard—both in terms of content, but also in terms of the emotional field they felt was present throughout. They ask if they heard, understood and summarized correctly.
- **FINE TUNE:** If the first person doesn't recognize what they said (or didn't like the way they said it), they can fine tune and explain.
- **SWITCH**
- **DISCUSS:** constructively, collaboratively, lovingly, without defensiveness or position-taking.

This felt a bit artificial at first, but for us it soon became a key monthly moment we were both equally attached to, especially when we started hitting some gravelly patches. It is comforting to learn you don't have to respond in the heat of the moment, when emotions are going to make you say something you shouldn't. You can do what all the mindfulness gurus in the world will teach you: breathe, observe the emotions elicited and their impact on you, the triggers that elicit them, and then calmly exchange this learning with your love. If you can build a culture of mutual curiosity, about both yourself and your other, you find that no subject is taboo. And instead of it becoming an issue between you, it becomes a way of learning more about each other, and how to best work and live to support each other. The liberation for both of us was in trusting the approach, and ourselves. We can both fall into being terribly polite and nice, which gets you quickly to shut down and resent what is unexpressed. We have gradually learned to trust that we can be radically honest with each other. And be heard. We learned we both felt massively better when we got whatever was bothering us off our chests, in a calm way. We could then think together how to resolve, address or simply digest it. It sounds absurdly simple, and isn't. It's deep and extremely powerful. Occasionally intense.

It also means you learn a certain kind of delayed gratification. It is wonderful to be able to vent, and complain or angst. But it can really wear on any relationship if there is too much of it, or it intrudes at inopportune moments when one or the other is not prepared or open to it. Having a regular date in the calendar (e.g. the first Sunday of the month) allows you to simply park it, knowing it will be addressed.

This approach is particularly beneficial in couples where one partner easily out-talks the other. It gives the quieter, or more introverted partner, a time and space to deliver somewhat prepared input. And forces the extrovert to listen carefully and respond. Both of us have grown to love these moments, even when they get into somewhat uncomfortable terrain. So far, we've been able to listen, learn and accept. It's also a good way to concentrate all the issues into a single sitting, so neither of you feels like you are constantly getting negative feedback. It minimises the number of times you address issues but maximises its impact. Which links it to the next and final ritual, which my husband insisted on, and is particularly good at.

FLATTERY

Okay, neither Tim nor I are the most attractive people on the planet. But to listen to us, you'd never know it. I am covered in a daily litany of compliments, showered with flattery, gazed at with admiration. Some I know have more or less of a grain of truth in them. But this hardly matters. It is heady stuff. Seriously cheap but potent perfume. And a delightful, daily blessing for a 55-year-old woman to be told on a daily basis she is gorgeous, sexy, brilliant and wise. I'm embarrassed to admit how much I enjoy hearing this. It makes me feel good inside, every time. Even though anyone could deservedly accuse him of repetition, exaggeration and outright lying, I know he believes it. Or at least thinks that if he repeats it enough, it will be true!

The science confirms Tim's strategy. It's called the five-to-one rule, and comes from John Gottman's research on happy marriages. It's a simple, statistical rule, as true at work as it is at home. The ideal proportion of positive to negative feedback is five nice things to one "constructive" thing. Compliments are just a good habit. Very few people use compliments as much as they could, especially not in longer-term relationships. We start losing the habit, getting too busy, taking each other a bit for granted as we focus on the "more important" matters at hand. And yet. There is probably nothing that contributes more to your happiness than the loving appreciation of your mate. Flavio, a Brazilian cousin of mine put it like this: 'I court my wife every day of out marriage' – and seeing them together, I believe him.

So don't be shy. Exaggerate. Amplify. Repeat. Learn the fine art of flattery. One of my favourite quotes comes from Christine Lagarde, long before she was head of the IMF. "If he is handsome, tell him he is intelligent. And if he is intelligent, tell him he is handsome." When done laughingly, wisely and well, soothing each other's respective insecurities with well-directed praise is what human genius was designed for.

MIRRORS

Mirrors and feminism don't quite go together. Or is feminism simply an escape from the unfair dictates of the image revealed by the mirror? Unattractive, and feminism becomes a haven for devoting your life to less superficial things. Too attractive, and it becomes an escape from the unwanted advances of people who judge books by their covers.

I got used, like most white, Western women, to hating my reflection quite young. I always liked food, and cooking. My favourite entertainment in the world is a lively dinner party with well-aged friends and wine. This leads to an inevitable battle of the bulge, mostly kept in check with a moderately disciplined devotion to the gym. I have followed the fashions of my eras, jogging when young enough not yet to have wrecked my hips, then Pilates, and now weekly yoga and a strange relationship with an elliptical machine. But I never quite got slim enough to consider myself attractive.

Until, that is, I fell in love again. Since I decided to throw my life and marriage on the line that New Year's Day, I couldn't find any objection to joining my office team's joint resolution to embark on some fad diet (Dukan, if you must know). A couple of months later, I had not only discovered the love of my later life, I'd also dropped the 10 pounds I'd always dreamt of losing. This, I know, I really do, should be an insignificant detail in this story. But it isn't.

The woman reflected in the eyes of my new man was someone I didn't know. She was gorgeous, sophisticated, well dressed. "Nubile," he gushes. She wore higher heels then I did, and much shorter skirts. She felt good about her body, appreciated the voluptuous lines and soft skin that her lover introduced her to, as though for the first time. She became used to her man endlessly caressing her curves in sighing admiration. She even began to enjoy her reflection in the mirror.

He made the same self-discovery. From self-effacing, lonely bachelor, dressed mostly in checks and browns, my admiring gaze fairy-godmothered him into a black-clad handsomeness that the mirror now laughingly tosses back at him. And my hands daily flatter the muscles of his back, bulk up his shoulders, elongate the slim legs. Bodies, and the daily attention to the physical, have become things we no longer take for granted – or ignore. The sense of touch has been promoted to its start-of-life pride of place. It has become a daily, loving ritual of mutual appreciation and gratitude. Every day begins – and ends – with languid, grateful kisses. The rest is detail.

In truth, the external transformation for both of us was probably relatively minor. Although I definitely wear higher heels. Friends comment on how well we look, in an indefinably enhanced sort of way. But it is the internal transformations that are radical. I discover that the old tropes about feeling good about yourself turn out to be violently true. You become the mirrored image you see in your loved one's gaze. It becomes the only truth. Then, inevitably, the other mirrors start to align, and other gazes start to see the same image.

Years ago, in the desolate days before my marriage officially ended, I fell into a mad though entirely unconsummated crush on a handsome man I worked with for a while. He was a big name. I fell for all his considerable qualities: his humour, his energy and, undeniably, his immaculate good looks. In my life, I had never really fallen quite so cravenly for anyone. Certainly not someone so completely unattainable. Someone who could claim anyone he chose, and, I thought, probably did.

I credit this rather hopeless infatuation with my awakening, though. I had spent a year or more vaguely looking around at the men who inhabited my slice of the world. Could I find someone else if I left? Were there any attractive specimens out there for the taking? Or was I just fooling myself, like all the books said, with my siren song of soulmates? I had rather lost faith when suddenly this man shook me out of my dormant state and showed me that someone did exist who could make my mind bounce, my knees wobble and my heart ache. The only trouble was that I never believed I was any match. Not in a million years.

He called me up this New Year's Monday. "Was I happy?" he asked. He had just dropped his youngest son off on his plane back to the other side of the planet. His wife was miserable. Was he happy, I asked. "Ha!" he said, "I'm complicated, you know..." As I hung up the phone, it hit me like a hammer. He had just arrived at the place where I had been standing years ago, to the very day. Knowing that things had to change and reaching out for a partner to dance a new dance. I suddenly saw my reflection in his eyes. And she was gorgeous, attractive, mature.

And utterly unattainable.

INTENTIONAL (RE)DESIGN

One of the loveliest learnings from marriage I have read comes from coach and speaker Gerald Rogers.[58] Rogers was left by his wife of 16 years, and the day he received the divorce papers, he sat down and listed the things he would do differently the next time around. He labelled this his "Marriage Advice I Wish I Would Have Had," and it went viral. If everyone followed his advice fewer first marriages might fail. For those entering later love relationships, his words are invaluable. The richness of late love is the potential to learn from the mistakes you made in earlier relationships. Here's an edited version:

1. ***Never stop courting****. Never stop dating. NEVER EVER take that woman for granted … She is the most important and sacred treasure you will ever be entrusted with. SHE CHOSE YOU. Never forget that, and NEVER GET LAZY in your love.*

2. ***Protect your own heart****. Just as you committed to being the protector of her heart, guard your own with the same vigilance. Love yourself fully, love the world openly, but there is a special place in your heart where no one must enter except your wife.*

3. ***Fall in love over and over again****. You will constantly change. You're not the same people you were when you got married, and in five years you will not be the same person you are today. Change will come, you must re-choose each other every day.*

4. ***Always see the best****. Focus only on what you love. What you focus on will expand. If you focus on what bugs you, all you will see is reasons to be bugged.*

5. ***It's not your job to change or fix her****. Your job is to love her as she is, with no expectation of her ever changing. And if she changes, love what she becomes, whether it's what you wanted or not.*

6. ***Take full accountability for your own emotions****: It's not your wife's job to make you happy, and*

---

58   http://geraldrogers.com/marriage-advice-i-wish-i-would-have-had/

she CAN'T make you sad. You are responsible for finding your own happiness, and through that your joy will spill over into your relationship and your love.

7. **Be present**. *Give her not only your time, but your focus, your attention and your soul. Do whatever it takes to clear your head so that when you are with her you are fully WITH HER. Treat her as you would your most valuable client. She is.*

8. **Be vulnerable.** *You don't have to have it all together. Be willing to share your fears and feelings, and quick to acknowledge your mistakes.*

9. **Never stop growing together**. *The stagnant pond breeds malaria, the flowing stream is always fresh and cool. Atrophy is the natural process when you stop working a muscle, just as it is if you stop working on your relationship. Find common goals, dreams and visions to work towards.*

10. **Always choose love.** *ALWAYS CHOOSE LOVE.*

THE TOOLKIT

Now is the time to reap the fruits of all you've sown. Greater self-awareness, a new and willing partner, and the future are all calling you to attention. It's time to consciously design, together, the kind of relationship you want to enjoy in this latter part of life. You are both old enough and wise enough to avoid past mistakes, and here are a few suggestions to make it – and keep it – growing and mutually enriching over time. Remember that love is an art form, and mastery a daily practice.

PAUSING BEFORE LEAPING

How do you start your day? Does it nourish or drain you? Energise or exhaust? In *The Artist's Way*,[59] Julia Cameron suggests to anyone interested in unleashing their creativity that they should write three longhand pages of "mind dump" every morning. It's very effective to clear your mind of clutter and negative voices and tap into a focus on priorities. You may want to use this technique to dream up and create your life's art form: your romantic relationship tripod: you, your partner, and the relationship itself.

---

59 Julia Cameron, *The Artist's Way: A Course in Discovering and Recovering Your Creative Self,* Macmillan, 2016

THREE THINGS

Each night, just before turning off the light, share the three things that most marked or delighted you during your day. It is a lovely way to tap into what has touched your partner's heart and mind, while enhancing a general sense of gratitude and attention to the positive. The positivity research has proven the benefits of intentionally focusing on the good things; it builds resilience and mutual appreciation. It also primes you for a very pleasant descent into slumber.

STRUCTURED, MONTHLY TALKS

Set aside an hour for a quiet conversation, e.g. the first Sunday of the month. Take turns doing a review of everything experienced during the month. Stick to the rules explained on page 146.

FLATTERY

The five to one rule: five compliments for every complaint, request or criticism. Or, as my cousin Flavio says: "Every day I woo my wife, and never take for granted I have won her."

WATCH THE ROLES YOU ADOPT

Do you unconsciously default to taking over certain roles in your couple? Evaluate this honestly and ask yourself if the roles need redesigning. Roles can be both internal and external.

- **External**: money-earner, parent, social organiser, cook, handyman, take-out-the-garbage person, vacation-planner, etc. Do you switch or do you stick? Is this consciously designed, or is there role fatigue on either side?

- **Internal**: peace-maker, moody person, happy person, keeper-of-the-peace, driver, innovator, challenger, weaker, stronger, change agent. How do these roles serve your couple, and are they limiting or growing each individual?

We tend to take on roles without thinking about it too much, and then get stuck into doing them forever. You may want to address this and intentionally take turns at some of them. I know I am seen as the "happy" one in my couple and Tim the moody one. And yet sometimes I am sad and down too, and I need his support, not his surprise, when something is bothering me. It's also my own problem, as I have trouble opening up to vulnerability and sadness. I need some encouragement and permission. Tim enjoys a full and fluid range of emotions, but tends to get stuck taking out the garbage. Talking about and acknowledging these habits is a key part of being able to change them. Sometimes just mentioning it makes change happen.

WHAT TO SHARE, WHAT TO KEEP

As important as it is to have common interests, most couples also spoke to me of how important it was to keep time for themselves. What are the two things you most love to do together and how often do you do it? What do you need to do on your own, and how often do you get to do it?

	1.	2.
DO TOGETHER		
DO ON MY OWN		

LEARNING NEW THINGS, TOGETHER

As important as it is to find your own space, it's also important to continue to learn and grow together. Research by Arthur Aron (of the Fall-in-Love questions)[60] indicates that happy couples try new adventures in neutral territory that belongs to neither of the two. The key ingredient is that it be a bit more exciting and out of the ordinary than just the usual, pleasant sharing of time. Tim and I have taken up dancing lessons, a hilarious get-together of a mixed bag of people in our local community hall a couple of nights a week. A Frenchman calls Jean shepherds us through "Le Rock & Roll." While our aging brains struggle to remember the steps, our happy bodies are energised by playing – and growing – in tandem.

---

60 Arthur Aron, *Shared Activities and Marital Satisfaction: Causal Direction and Self-Expansion versus Boredom,* 1993 http://journals.sagepub.com/doi/abs/10.1177/026540759301000205?journalCode=spra

BOOKS

Terrence Real, *The New Rules of Marriage: What You Need to Know to Make Love Work,* Ballantine Books, 2008

I am a big admirer of Terrence Real. He is one of the only relationship experts I have read who integrates gender differences into his analysis of the state of contemporary relationships in a knowledgeable and powerful way. He boils down the current state of affairs to a simple statement: "In the last generation women have radically changed and men, by and large, have not." If you agree with this, or it echoes your own relationship's lack of balance, this will be a crucial read. He is an expert in male depression (an earlier book of his), and brings his deep understanding of how men's emotional range has been limited by 20th-century social forces and how this still impacts 21st-century relationships.

Eli Finkel, *The All or Nothing Marriage, 2017.*

Finkel takes a scientist's approach to studying the advent of an era boasting some of the happiest marriages the world has ever seen. And expectations to match.

Gary Chapman, *The Five Love Languages: The Secret to Love that Lasts,* Northfield Publishing, 2015

Chapman explains that different people want to be loved – and shown they are loved – in different ways. We each have a strong preference for a particular one of five love languages: words of affirmation, quality time, receiving gifts, acts of service, physical touch. Mine is words of affirmation, hence the "flattery" section above, Tim's is touch. People run into trouble because they tend to offer support based on their own preference, rather than on that of their partner, which leads to a very different impact than was intended and may cause resentment. This is an easy one to explore and get right. A quick read with a big impact. Do it! Once you know what makes your partner's heart rejoice, you just dial up the dose, daily, in an infinite series of variations.

Esther Perel, *Mating in Captivity: Sex, Lies and Domestic Bliss,* Hodder & Stoughton, 2012

Perel describes both the staleness of sexual relations in modern egalitarian couples and the thirst for more passion. She suggests that people need to learn to balance commitment with excitement, security with risk, and embrace the inherent contradictions of what they are actually after.

VIDEOS

Esther Perel, *"The Secret to Desire in a Long-Term Relationship"*

https://www.ted.com/talks/esther_perel_the_secret_to_desire_in_a_long_term_relationship

A great TED Talk, watched by more than 10 million people, reflecting the current dissatisfaction with the status quo. "Can we want what we already have?" All about sex, desire and keeping the flame alive in committed relationships. She argues that individualism and romanticism kill desire. She names the two competing needs that battle away in our breasts: security vs. adventure, and offers suggestions on how to reconcile them by building "erotic intelligence."

Jane Fonda, *"Life's Third Act,"*

https://www.ted.com/talks/jane_fonda_life_s_third_act

The gorgeous and vibrant Fonda sharing her wisdom on getting the best of the extra 30 years of the longevity gift we have been granted. She quotes Picasso saying "it takes a long time to become young," and reiterates much of this book's suggestions: review the first two thirds of your life, understand what happened, and perhaps even change your relationship with the past to free your future from its clutches. "In our third acts, it may be possible for us to circle back to where we started, and know it for the first time."

Robert Waldinger, *"What Makes a Good Life?"*

https://www.ted.com/talks/robert_waldinger_what_makes_a_good_life_lessons_from_the_longest_study_on_happiness/transcript?language=en

Harvard has run the longest study of a single body of humans in the world. For 75 years, a class of 725 Harvard men (and eventually their wives) were followed physically, intellectually and emotionally by four different directors. The men are now in their 90s, and their lives have been studied bi-annually to see what makes lives work. In short: good relationships keep us happier, healthier and longer living, not fame or money. Quality relationships, especially with personal partners, seem to keep not only bodies and hearts, but also brains healthier into older age. So it's worth the work!

LEAPING

Potential to the Power of Two

"It's hard to overestimate the constructive power of love … The achievement of an intimate relationship empowers us. Feeling important to someone we are close to provides a sense of belonging and security, and the mutual recognition necessary to our self-validation."

Ethel Person

"Love adds a precious seeing to the eye."

Shakespeare

"That's how I conceive of love; it's a mutual understanding (a reciprocal pact?)
that the other's needs are close to equal—and in some cases more important—
than one's own. The result of this knowledge is a sense of safety; I'm never in this alone. In a
world full of uncertainties, the tacit commitment of another sentient individual
is reassuring and tremendously empowering."

My son

WHERE TO GO FROM LOVE

· ·

MIRACLES HAPPEN, and two people end up re-aligned with themselves and their intimate partner. Then what? Where do they go from there? Does the energy and self-belief that comes from being loving and well-loved echo out into the world? Or does it stay a purely private pleasure?

The surprise of love, writes the French philosopher Alain Badiou, "unleashes a process that is basically an experience of getting to know the world. Love isn't simply about two people meeting and their inward-looking relationship: it is a construction, a life that is being made, no longer from the perspective of One but from the perspective of Two… What is the world like when it is experienced, developed and lived from the point of view of difference and not identity? "[61]

Psychologist Jonathan Haidt says, "Some of the greatest joys in life come from nurturing and from what's called 'generativity.' People have a strong striving to build something, to do something, to leave something behind."[62] And these strivings are stoked and multiplied in late love couples.

I found that a happy, excitedly supportive partner at home really sparked my own appetite to work, to write, to take risks in new directions, like this book. Tim's astonishing ability to listen

---

61   Alain Badiou, *In Praise of Love,* Serpent's Tail, 2012
62   Interviewed in Aziz Ansari's *Modern Romance: An Investigation,* Penguin, 2016

allowed my extroverted self to think aloud over endless dinners with an engaged and intelligent sparring partner. His flattering admiration of my writing was invitation to share early drafts and get feedback and ideas—or just, I must admit, pure unadulterated admiration. It's good for the soul, and for the stamina to get through projects where you may not entirely believe in yourself. When your partner gazes at you in admiration, and tells you the idea is simply brilliant, for me it's pure engine fuel. Both heady and necessary. So many have written of the powerful fuel that love offers creativity:

"Joy, gladness, ecstasy, and love make us feel expansive, worthy, and important. These feelings too are empowering; they enhance our ability to reach out, to form bonds with others, to enter into new activities."[63]

"We can awaken in each other possibilities beyond our wildest dreams. The conversation of togetherness is a primal and indeed perennial conversation. Despite the thousands of years of human interaction, it all begins anew, as if for the first time, when two people fall in love. The force of their encounter makes a real clearance; through the power of Eros they discover the beauty in each other. Stretching the power of Eros they discover the beauty in each other. Stretching across the distance towards each other, they begin to awaken all the primal echoes where nothing can be presumed but almost everything can be expected."[64]

Our getting together enabled Tim to quit a job that he found unsatisfying, and return to the art and sculpture he had excelled at earlier on. As I write, I see him on the other side of the room, focused for hours on ideas he is dreaming up for his next project. He is happy, concentrated, in the flow. In large part, I know, this is because I do for him what he does for me: encourage, admire, applaud. I think he is a fabulous sculptor, and I love the soul behind the artistic striving that seeks to share its passion for life, and love and beauty. I encourage him to take the time, to make the space, to follow his passions and instincts. It is exciting and satisfying to watch him grow and reach further than he might have on his own. If not now, when? Is a central question for this latter phase of life.

---

63   Ethel Person, *Feeling Strong: How Power Issues Affect our Ability to Direct our Own Lives,* HarperCollins, 2003
64   John O'Donohue, *Beauty: The Invisible Embrace,* Harper Perennial, 2005

"There is nothing in a caterpillar that tells you it's going to be a butterfly."

R. Buckminster Fuller

This is the ideal we have both been after, of course. A partner who will give and take in equal measure in a determined commitment to mutual self-enhancement. I don't know why people still seem to consider this a selfish goal for people unhappily sitting on the fence in unsatisfactory relationships. As a coach, I have seen so often, consistently and repeatedly, that people do their best work, their best contribution of their talents to the world, when they are finally ready to listen and respond to the inner voice trying to tell them the truth about themselves—and when they have the right kind of support from key people in their lives. There are a million quotes, which I love to collect, about doing what you are meant to be doing in the world. My favorite is the Gerard Manley Hopkins poem that Tim has carved into the base of one of his sculptures, two abstract arms reaching to the sky, that sits in our garden:

As Kingfishers Catch Fire
Gerard Manley Hopkins

As kingfishers catch fire, dragonflies draw flame;
As tumbled over rim in roundy wells
Stones ring; like each tucked string tells, each hung bell's
Bow swung finds tongue to fling out broad its name;
Each mortal thing does one thing and the same:
Deals out that being indoors each one dwells;
Selves — goes itself; myself it speaks and spells,
Crying What I do is me: for that I came.

By permission of Oxford University Press from THE PEOMS OF GERARD MANLY HOPKINS, 4E edited by W.H. Gardner and N.H MacKenzie, 1967, 1970.

While some may feel such opportunities to be oneself are for a privileged few, there is within the general unlocking of late love—emotional, intellectual, sexual—a creative energy that comes bubbling out with the rest. What you then do with it, and whether you will bubble together into new projects, or fuel each other's ambitions in older ones, is much of the unexpected fun of late love.

Robert's sudden falling in love entirely changed his life at the age of 57. His younger wife's natural belief that "anything is possible" starkly contrasted with his own inherited position, the child of two working-class parents of the 1950s, that nothing was. A successful businessman, he had buried himself in work after an early marriage to a career-oriented woman failed decades earlier. Late love transformed him from a lonely, workaholic coming home to an empty house, to a father of three, coming home to a bustling, loving home and the ecstatic cries of a welcoming toddler. "I can barely fathom the man I was just a few years ago. My life has been so utterly transformed." His wife has become someone who "drags him over new thresholds." He works less, and has invested enormously in fatherhood in a way he wasn't able to when his first daughter, now 26, was born. "For my first wife, children were a problem to be solved. Now, for both of us, they are a joy to behold." Every day, the couple makes time and space to share—ideas, emotions, fears. For Robert, this kind of daily support is giving him wings. He is becoming more open to creative forces of all kinds—going to festivals, making videos for his business, writing his own autobiography to make sure his children know him, as he is clear-eyed about his own mortality. Contemplation and conversation has replaced the workaholic rut he had let himself get stuck in.

When Marie married Richard in 2008, he was already retired and she was at her professional peak. He delightedly drove her around the US to conferences where she spoke and sold her books. "I enjoyed a feeling of stability I never had before," says Marie. "I have a new ability to enjoy life, it's the first time I feel really secure." This eventually allowed her to shift from a very successful career as a teacher of writing and a trainer of writing teachers, to becoming a full-time poet herself at age 60. Now, their life is a balance of writing, exercising and the dancing they have enjoyed since their first date.

But first things first. Before you redesign life work and purpose, there are first the inevitable building blocks to (re)establishing as a couple in later life. For most, some of the immediate priorities are the most obvious: cities, homes, families, and the question of weddings. I place them in the order in which they often emerge.

After these basics, these new couples can become creative powerhouses, whether it's in entrepreneurship, philanthropy, volunteering or simply social glue; whether it's together or apart, these re-energised couples can have a big impact on the world around them. But first, some basics.

OF CULTURE AND COUNTRIES

While this issue may not apply to many couples, the increased mobility of recent decades means it is relevant for an increasing number. Couples where each half comes from different countries face the choice of what country they can or want to live in. Tim is British and has spent only a few years living outside of his home country. I am a mix of Canadian and French and spent most of my adult life in Continental Europe. He joined me in Paris for a year while my daughter finished high school. Then I moved in with him in London. We were both shocked by a Brexit vote that made our choice slightly less obvious (at least to me) than it had been before. This will certainly cause years of confusion among thousands of bi-national couples. Interestingly, residency is not automatically granted to spouses in the UK, but it is in France. So we may yet move back, or at least that's what I tease Tim about when I am disgruntled with the latest in British politics.

These are the added complexities of millions of cross-border couples. Family considerations obviously come into play. Where your parents are, where your children are. It's complicated! Some choose a neutral third country, some are constrained by work options, or by pension currencies. If they can afford it, some keep one foot in more than one country.

We have decided to stick to the wonders of multi-cultural London for the moment. Family and friends love to visit, and we have nested deeply into the fabric of our neighborhood and our city. But I have renewed my French passport, and added Tim to my "*Carnet de Famille*," the family document that each French citizen carries through life that lists all the children you have, and all the men you marry!

As I write, the French have elected a new President, Emmanuel Macron, whose wife is 24 years his senior. This is a total contrast to Donald Trump and his wife who is 24 years his junior. The stereotypes and their reversals are hilarious indicators of the cultures of each country around love and coupling. And the two couples represent drastically different role models of what late love looks like. Vive la différence!

Just don't assume anything. Life is long, political turbulence on the menu for decades to come, and the discussion of where to live for mixed couples is worth exploring. An open mind and a lot of geographical flexibility on both sides may be a huge benefit.

My Window

Some writers choose to face a wall. I went for a window. It is a big Georgian job, with 16 panes, and a couple of hundred years worth of views. A tiny desk, reserved for the treasured and disciplined writing hours, is tucked into its recess. The bottom four panes frame a festive run of flowering city gardens and small, brick workers' homes. It's all green and brick and chimney pots, even now in the middle of January, with a cherry tree in gorgeous and scarily untimely blossom. Just above the cosy quadrangle towers an ever upward-thrusting row of glass and steel. They glint and shine, day and night, flaunting the glittering ambitions of the global city of London beyond the wall.

The top 12 panes are filled with sky. At the bottom, the slow, seasonal cycles battle it out with the ever-more-ravenous appetites of capitalism's encroaching maw. At the top, a very Jungian call to a higher self. Today, it's a perfectly bright blue up there, interrupted only by the rhythmic passage of planes, a reminder of what awaits me soon enough: work and women and world affairs. You can't escape those bottom panes, bringing you down to earth.

Today, though, the blue pulls me outside. I learned quickly that in this island city, the clouds arrive before lunch on even the most perfect mornings. In the hubbub of London life, a morning walk is my favourite mise en bouche for the day, but requires careful calibration. Too early, and you are swamped by the million commuters barrelling along the South Bank. Then the walk becomes an inhospitable reminder of your general outlier status, as you dare to stroll amidst the self-important rush of people going places. Too late, and you dodge between the Lycra-clad joggers and the lunchtime crowd.

Around 9.30 though, there is a sweet spot of about two hours, between the getting-to-work and the getting-to-lunch. A few solitary souls are sprinkled, slowed by the sudden generosity of space, or the astonishing beauty of the view. The pace, nearing quiet, lets me admire the skyline I waltzed into some years ago, from another country, another life. I didn't walk every day there, I didn't see the need. I was still a wife, a mother, a boss. I still needed to be busy. I didn't look up too much, didn't find a window there. Eventually, I found the door.

Now, I'm increasingly mesmerized by the view from the upper panes. While friends become addicted to the latest TV series, and everywhere everyone calls for connection, I am drawn to my 12-paned expanse of airy beauty. It is not stillness. There is a constant, driving energy here. Its power feels immense. Love, too, is in this air. The wind is in love with the clouds, the seagulls swoon together on high, the plane is rushing to meet her sun. And heaven's eyes, for me, are blue. That deep, deep blue that catches you as you fall. Like all the loves in my life, blue-eyed all.

HOME AND HEART

Whose home to live in? Will he move in to her home, or will she move into his? Will they stay in living-together-apart, each in their own homes, or will they buy a new home together? There are as many solutions as there are couples. Space, color, design and functionality are fascinating keys into any couple's dynamics.

Aileen and her new partner, David, have been together for nine years but still work and live in different cities. They have bought a house together where they will retire within the next few years; David has time to fix it up while Aileen works the last few years before her retirement. They are designing and decorating it together. "Our lifestyle, splitting homes as we do, may seem strange to some," she says. "We don't have to be together in the evenings and we have separate bedrooms and our own space. I've always wanted that, and he sees it as a positive. My family sees it as an indication that we are not committed. It's a bit out of the norm, and I like that. It allows me solitude, which makes me happier in the relationship. My good friends see it as perfect, especially if they are married!"

I moved into Tim's lovely London home. But he immediately wanted to repaint and reorganize the house to make it "ours." We did two rounds of this, one immediately, and once again four years in. He moved his studio out of the house and into a bigger shared artist place nearby, and built me a pantry off the kitchen. I have an office at home, which we share, and Tim built a long, sleek desk dotted with our two laptops and matching chairs. We share a love of design and spent months carefully negotiating a style that melds our preferences, colors and new use of space.

After only two years together, David and Elisabeth stick to their hard-won comfort with independence, and live in their respective, much-loved homes a five-minute walk apart. "Part of our design is she says 'I want to be alone today, is that OK?' and I always say yes. I want her to realise her dream life. If either of us need alone time, that is not less loving, it is more loving to have space." One of David's favorite places to be on the planet is sitting in one of the two wing-backed chairs in front of Elisabeth's fireplace, contentedly talking and sharing their days.

Andrea moved into Mark's house because it was bigger and he still had his two sons at home. Then they spent months renovating and designing the top floor to make room for Andrea's grown children when they visited and hanging Andrea's art on the walls. They also commissioned some art together, to expand her passion into a shared adventure.

The constant among all these stories is the desire for a balance between shared, inclusive space for both styles and functions, combined with a need for one's own independent space. The intentional inclusion of each other's "stuff," the meaningful artefacts of two pasts coming together, is something I think about a lot. Whether this involves the melding of physical space or not, it is certainly a melding together of the geography of the time you spend together. Small, meaningful rituals get created, like Elisabeth's cup of tea in front of the fire, or our approach to bicycles.

TOWARDS TANDEMS

We come with baggage, of course. And bicycles.

On the one hand, there is an old, rather basic racing bike, appropriately labelled "Londoner." It is dark and rather dirty, maybe once black. It has weathered many a year, like my man, accompanying him on commuting trips to work, to art college, or to his beloved bronze foundry. It has been the steadiest of companions all these years, and he settles onto its saddle with satisfaction, knowing his boundless energy will now be put to good use, propelling him forward towards his next task.

My Londoner loves his city, and is a pure product of its busy, doing culture. He likes direction, and purpose and the effort of leaning into the wind to get there. Like his father, he is passionate about many things, and gets a bit breathless trying to squeeze too many into this single bike ride on Earth.

He has also, like most of us, had times where he has been completely knocked from the saddle. More than his fair share, I think. But no matter how far he has fallen, he is the sort of Londoner who resolutely gets back on, determined to pedal anew. Life is measured in accomplishments, and duty, and he is British after all.

I, on the other hand, expend undue amounts of energy staying in place. My bike is an elliptical exercise thing, whose sole purpose is to allow its owner to enjoy eating as much as she likes while only moderately suffering the consequences. It also reflects my natural leanings and laziness. I love to live in the present. I enjoy the 30 minutes I regularly spend on this thing, stuck in a corner of the garden, covered by the lovely roof that my love has built to protect me from the harsh shock of British weather. I feel little need to get anywhere, and spend most of my time trying to figure out who I am, rather than where I'm headed.

One could conclude that these two energies are impossibly contradictory. One thrusting energetically forward, the other tenaciously holding in place. But instead, we've found a new symbol, one that brings both together in the most delightful way. It's a bike that Tim bought decades ago, when he was still in university, and dreaming of riding through life as an ideal couple. It's a tandem, of course. And it has – finally – found its time and purpose.

It is perfect. Tim will ride in front, head bent down, facing the elements, finding purpose and direction, fighting the turbulent winds, real and metaphorical, that the world will throw our way. I will not-so-demurely ride behind, and admire the scenery, let myself be transported (most pleasantly and gallantly) forward and write about the experience…

FAMILIES

The melding of families is usually a major part of late love. The key issue is children, of course. Will they approve, or even rejoice? Or will they deny and refuse and sprinkle toxic fumes over their parent's tentative reach for happiness? In Kent Haruf's *Our Souls at Night*, the mother's inspiring late love is destroyed by her son's anger and disgust. But in most of the interviews I conducted, children, on the whole, were delighted to see their parents tumble into happiness.

Robert was estranged from his daughter for a decade when he remarried. But when his daughter heard he was expecting a new baby, she came to visit, and from there gradually reinstated her position in central casting as the child of a now-happy family. Robert delightedly says he has never been closer to her, a development he hadn't dreamt of achieving just a couple of years earlier. She is enjoying being big sister to the new babies, and finds her new stepmother can support and connect with her in ways her own could not. While children may often suffer the collateral damage of bad divorces, they can also find unexpected solace in the happiness of redesigned families, a story that is largely untold.

Lisa also got unexpectedly closer to her daughter after she married Marc. Her daughter, an ambitious working woman, lived on the other side of the country, and married and had kids late. "Since she's had kids of her own, we have gotten very close. My late husband was so demanding of me and my time, I couldn't have had this time with the kids. Marc doesn't care what I do, he says 'do whatever you want.'" This Lisa has a newly discovered sense of freedom, and is discovering the joys of dedicated time with her own children.

Andrea hesitated for years before leaving her husband, fearing for her children and reluctant to bear the wrath she expected from them. And yet, five years later, at her second wedding, her eldest daughter gave a toast that brought tears to everyone's eyes. She thanked her new stepfather for transforming her mother into the confident, laughing and loving woman she had become. If ever there was a moment that validated her mother's difficult choices, it was this one, as the newly formed family celebrated their parent's decisions—and publicly appreciated the reasons and the result. And the result has had profound implications for her daughters' view of their own love lives. Growing up, watching the daily debacle that was their parents' marriage, they were understandably cynical about marriage, and convinced they would not wed. Yet now, seeing their own mother so happy and energized by a powerfully constructive partner, they are warming up in their own relationships. They can start to invest them with a future they can now envisage, having watched it blossom in the inner parts of their own mother's heart. Talk about role modeling! Ironic that Andrea waited so long to leave when, in the end, leaving and loving has been probably one of the most important gifts she will have given her girls.

When Martha and Richard announced their intention to marry, one of his sons accepted, the other wouldn't even talk to his father. "I would rather be a foot soldier in Iraq than be at your wedding," was his only comment. Richard didn't wait for approval. "I was hurt, but I kept calm and carried on, knowing that I had to let these feelings play out over time." This son eventually asked his brother whether Martha "told him what to do, and whether he called her mom," revealing all the often unspoken fears that inhabit children facing remarriages. Time and steadiness worked their magic and when Richard turned 60, his son sent him 60 reasons why he loved him, one of which was "you gave me enough time to get over mom's death."

Nothing is more key to a relationship than the successful navigation of the challenges of integrating children into the equation. The more time and thought and effort are put into it, the more likely everyone will find their place. Children want to know they still come first in their respective parents' hearts. This needs to be clear from the start. And not only in the children's minds, but also in the heart of your partner.

Creating new family rituals and ceremonies and holidays is a key part of the design phase of late love. How much time and attention will be made for the broader family? How, when and where will they be integrated? Who needs what from whom? Will children, siblings and parents have rooms of their own in your lives and in your hearts?

When Tim and I got together we each still had one parent alive, both in their 90s. Both were able to attend our wedding, and were quick to bless our union. We have been lucky. My mother's approval was incredibly important to me. Her immediate, non-judgmental welcoming of Tim into the family was a huge relief. She and my first husband had a good relationship; I am delighted that it is matched equally by her relationship with Tim. Tim's father was hugely relieved to see his bachelor son finally rewarded with a wife. He himself had adored his own wife and couldn't quite fathom why his beloved son couldn't find a match. This parental approval is balm to the soul of any loving child, and we have been twice blessed.

It is the same with my kids. You so desperately want them to—if not exactly understand your choice—at least acknowledge it has led to a better place. Children are neither stupid nor selfish. While the ride may be rough, and you may feel you are losing one or the other of your kids for a while, your own sense of self will be what convinces them in the end. Your own happiness is potently convincing to those who love you. When my children and my mother saw me with Tim, they understood what I had not been particularly skilled at putting into words. The slightly hardened carapace I had built around me made me a bit tough, sarcastic and occasionally confrontational. I morphed, almost immediately, into a much softer version of me—full of laughter, happiness and a deep, boundless gratitude. Being loved, I loved all the more, and all the better, and spread it ever further around.

How could my children not see—and appreciate—the change? It warmed their hearts as it had warmed mine. That's what happiness does. It spreads and infects those around you just as surely as its opposite. We are closer than we have ever been. They nestle into the happiness of our new home, grateful in their turn to the man who made their mother laugh so girlishly—and so often. It also helps, of course, that Tim had a lovely home in central London, good taste, and competence in a vast range of areas where I have none. Children do appreciate a well-placed and well-serviced *pied-a-terre* in chic, global cities. But he also has a very different personality type from mine; he is more compassionate, far more volatile in his moods, and endlessly more empathetic to all. He is, in fact, much closer in many ways to my daughter, and can better accompany, listen and help her tame some of her anxieties than I can. There are few things I find more touching about my late love than to watch my up-to-now childless husband spending hours on the phone with one or the other kid (last week it was the better part of a day debugging a new laptop that was about to cause a major breakdown).

And for Tim, one of the unexpected pleasures of our late love is the gift of parenthood. He relishes having suddenly been catapulted into the highly emotional and ever-changing front-row seat at the spectacle of two young people emerging in the world. And not only them. Suddenly his one-time aging bachelor pad is filled with the sounds (and smells!) of whole bunches of millennials – my kids' friends - swooping in and out like swallows for holidays, celebrations or just a good meal (they are also open to hand-me-downs, old iPhones and any bottles of wine we don't mind parting with). His pristine house is often littered with sleeping bags and the neighbours must wonder at the sudden increase in passionate, night-long philosophical debates in the garden. He delights in playing the wise elder to a range of my kids' friends only too eager to get a bit of advice or just a mature, listening ear. Young adults are such a bracing call to keep step with the world. And Tim, who was slowly retreating into the more isolated fields of old friends and workaholism, is suddenly surrounded. Our kids and their friends are a constant ebullient invitation to stay awake and open to tomorrow. Their tomorrow.

For me, watching these new relationships form and grow is transformative in so many ways I can barely keep up. Watching my new husband with my children and my children with him is an ode to love. We are always at choice about whether to allow love into our lives. Whether children can receive it from someone new, someone they have not chosen. Whether we can give it to someone else's children, and love them as our own. Watching the handful of humans I love most in the world accept and learn to love each other, mostly because they love me, routinely moves me to tears. And then it catches, like a flame, and they are off in their own relationships, independent of me, playing in their own affinities, enlarging the family circle, teaching me, again and again, how to love. I left and loved anew in part because I thought I had something to teach them. In the end, they are teaching me.

THE EMPTY NEST ADJUSTMENT

Your skin still crawls with vigilance. Your ear awaits the daily cacophony of demands. And then abruptly, the suns you've been circling stop and everything is infinitely silent. The little one left for college in September. I'm not one of those who grieve at this turn of events. I love it. I've long planned for it, and redesigned my own life, and love, in anticipation, years ago. I could sing from the rooftops with pride and curiosity and admiration for the humans my not-too-turbulent teens have turned into. I could also crow at the freedom flowing from the space their leaving has opened up.

And yet, old habits take time to loosen their grip. Life was always so full. I would wake wondering how to squeeze things in, and go to sleep prioritising the morrow. An empty moment was as rare as a tidy room. My muscles were primed for the daily marathon of modern motherhood, which is a largely cerebral balancing act between the competing demands of the world, work and the womb. Relentlessly intense.

Now, I do yoga. Daily. The demands of only-work seem a paltry thing compared to decades of stretching between conflicting voices. I often felt like a cherry pie, with everyone avid for a slice. A weekend without kids is a whole new kind of vacation. There is nothing to do but entertain yourself.

It takes quite a lot of getting used to. You are always waiting for a new need, you try and keep plans flexible, just in case.

For the first few months it makes sense. You become a transitional hand to hold as one moves to college, the other through a job transition. I've had weeks with daily calls and occasional tears. I've been called in to edit this or that. When there is outrage at being reprimanded by a manager, or still-shaking fear from a car accident, you revisit the sleepless nights of yore. But all that, I know, is coming to its natural end. No news is, literally, good news. The more the little stars shine, the less you are likely to hear about it.

As I almost imperceptibly relax into this new reality, I discover an entirely new phase of life is on offer at 55. In many ways, it resembles my 22-year-old son's. Recently graduated, he is exploring the world and his own place in it. He has a decade to learn and play before he may choose to settle on who he is and what he wants to serve. I also feel recently graduated, with a graduate degree in parenting and the First-Half-of-Life. I also have a decade or so to learn and experiment with what I have become and what I want to serve in my second act. I feel, a lot like him, that I can do anything I put my mind to. With the advantage of having already done it a few times.

I will, I know, write more books, and lean in and give back, and delight in supporting the next generation in their journeys. But just now, just for a year, I've given myself some time to adjust. It's a bigger change than I thought. I wonder if astronauts feel like this as they catapult through constellations of space and abruptly end up with their feet firmly planted back on Mother Earth. Back where you started, but it's unrecognisable, as you are seeing it all with an entirely new set of eyes and a heart that has glimpsed magnitudes.

WEDDINGS

"Marriage is a fine institution, but I'm not ready for an institution."

Mae West

To wed or not to wed? Most late love couples will dance around this question at some point. Some will because one or both of you yearn to embed your commitment in public, in law or simply in celebration. Others do because it will be essential to guarantee the health, wealth or sustainability of your partner once one of you dies, depending on the legislation of the country in which you reside. For some, it is hugely meaningful, for others purely administrative. Whether there is a legal component or not, most of the couples I interviewed marked their commitment to each other with some kind of an event, large or small. A lot of pleasure and meaning came from celebrating the joy that late love had unleashed, and sharing that with one's community, large or small, was seen as a delightful dance.

Late weddings aren't like the first time round. They are less pressured, more relaxed and in many ways more profound. Both partners have been around, as have many of their guests. Children are often present, adding a layer of complexity and witnessing that is particularly probing. You are entering territory you may have already navigated, and learned something of survival skills and what you need for the journey. It is a trip you embark on, this time, with your eyes wide open. If, that is, you've been there before.

Marc and Lisa decided not to wed legally for a variety of financial and inheritance issues, and Lisa felt awkward getting married for what seemed a somewhat exaggerated third time. Instead, they simply designed a deeply meaningful wedding ceremony – without the legalities. Their eyes still shine when they describe it. They wrote a typical Jewish ceremony, sat under the chuppah, and instead of the ritual of the groom circling the bride seven times, they had their combined grandchildren circle round them. "I feel married," says Lisa, "I feel like a kid again, we have such a good time. I have a tremendous sense of freedom. Our former spouses were the type to do one thing a day. Now, Marc and I live in downtown Manhattan and we do twelve things a day."

Tim had never been married, so our wedding, five years after we linked lives, was his first. For him, it was a celebration of what he had looked for all his life and had not been able to find. The poem, by David Whyte, that he read at our wedding, was so powerfully true it hurt (see next page).

The Truelove

David Whyte

There is a faith in loving fiercely
the one who is rightfully yours,
especially if you have
waited years and especially
if part of you never believed
you could deserve this
loved and beckoning hand
held out to you this way.

I am thinking of faith now
and the testaments of loneliness
and what we feel we are
worthy of in this world.

Years ago in the Hebrides,
I remember an old man
who walked every morning
on the grey stones
to the shore of baying seals,

who would press his hat
to his chest in the blustering
salt wind and say his prayer
to the turbulent Jesus
hidden in the water,

and I think of the story
of the storm and everyone
waking and seeing
the distant,
yet familiar figure
far across the water
calling to them,
and how we are all
waiting for that
abrupt waking,
and that calling,
and that moment
we have to say *yes*,

except, it will
not come so grandly,
so Biblically,
but more subtly
and intimately, in the face
of the one you know
you have to love.

So that when
we finally step out of the boat
toward them, we find
everything holds
us, and everything confirms
our courage, and if you wanted
to drown you could,
but you don't,
because finally
after all this struggle
and all these years,
you don't want to any more,
you've simply had enough
of drowning,

and you want to live and you
want to love and you will
walk across any territory
and any darkness,
however fluid and however
dangerous, to take the
one hand you know
belongs in yours.

Printed with permission from Many Rivers Press,
www.davidwhyte.com.
David Whyte, True Love, title of source book,
©Many Rivers Press, Langley, WA USA

For me, the wedding was a celebration of all I had dared to dream, and succeeded in claiming by sheer stubborn belief and hope—in myself, in Tim, in my family. I had dared to make a dash for, and been so amply rewarded in the finding, the supposedly mythical, but now very tangible reality of my handsome, joyous and beaming soul-mate.

GETTING MARRIED (AGAIN)

It was lovely and light, the second time around. Riding on a double-decker bus to Brixton Town Hall, a hastily bought bunch of yellow roses, a sunny lunch with two old friends-cum-witnesses. It was like the frothy foam on a cappuccino – as airy and light as the base was deep and intense.

But becoming legal was only the hors d'oeuvre. It was quickly swallowed by the planning for the subsequent wedding party, a month further along. If we managed to stay married until the party, it was a minor miracle. There was something in this event that brought out – and magnified – the extremes in our respective styles. The man threw himself into wedding fever with a vengeance, and spent the better part of most days on some aspect of getting wed. It was, after all, his first time. I was wedded to the idea of simplicity. It was, after all, my second.

I had somehow imagined an extension of our Town Hall turn. A light get-together of old friends, a toast to our good health, and a few balloons thrown in for good measure. Instead, I got 90 guests, 120 bottles of champagne, 180 glasses, 300 balloons, 450 canapes, 250 bruschettas, 450 dessert bijoux, as well as a double-decker wedding cake, two outfits for me, a new suit for him and shoes-to-go-with for the both of us. They call it wedding inflation. We paid in cash. It almost caused a marital crash.

My new spouse saw his two usually charming attributes go into overdrive: perfectionism and putting others first. I loosely proposed a few songs around which we could weave some toasts, scribbled on a page while visiting my mom. He started writing out detailed interventions for friends and family in a Powerpoint presentation. He worried what people would think, and eat, and drink. I ordered lime green balloons. He plumbed his passion for Jane Austen into a series of carefully selected cinematic excerpts to illustrate how I resembled her, or at least her heroines. Then timed every song and speech to the minute only to discover that we had an hour and a half of self-serving celebration that would soon make any self-respecting wedding guest thoroughly sick of love – at least our kind. He danced across outline after outline … after outline, drawing me into what felt, to my informal, spontaneous self, like a deadly dance of detail. Until I, too, became thoroughly sick of love, and welcomed work as an escape hatch out of the house – and the to-do list. A former event planner, even he began to admit that getting married was beginning to feel as stressful as the job he had left...

What is it, we wondered, that was propelling us so far from the serene, mutual adoration in which we had sailed through our first five years together? And our shared goal of an unassuming-but-romantic exchange of vows in front of a loving community of friends?

Partly it was peer pressure. We had invited our dearest friends, a lifetime of linkages now liberally sprinkled across the globe. We didn't expect most of them to care enough about us to travel. But they did, from 14 different countries. Flattering, it immediately raised the stakes. They care! So we must take care of them, in turn. Nourish and entertain them, entrance them with our story and our choices and our love.

Then my girlfriends began to ask what I was wearing. I had bought a cute faux-leather cream-coloured dress from Zara that I thought was the perfect aging-lady ironic take on a wedding dress, complete with a nod to my still-tortured relationship with the money-clothing-vanity trilogy that undermines too many women and girls (did I say weddings are light-hearted?). My friends did not approve. It didn't seem to quite live up to what they felt I should invest in that sweep down an aisle I hadn't yet imagined having.

Another friend, fashion industry savvy, volunteered to take the man shopping for a suit. She generously asked me if I was intending to join them. I figured out why pretty quickly when she led us to Savile Row (my discount store preferences are well-known to my uber-fashionable friends). As he (rather handsomely) paraded about in an undeniably chic purple suit, I wondered what his old friends would make of this new image, including its £1200 price tag. In the end, he couldn't bite that particular bullet, and so we went shopping alone the following weekend, surreptitiously settling for more Zara. He still looked drop-dead gorgeous. The rest was detail.

But the getting there left us wounded and exhausted. Despite our best intentions, we just couldn't seem to find a way to work together to make the planning of this celebration any fun, despite an insightful coach-friend's taking pity on us and preventively analysing our very different decision-making styles. My man liked or needed to worry and plan and spend a lot of time on every aspect. I did not. He thrives on detail, I throttle on it. He likes to prepare, I like to wing it. He says tomato, I say tomato…

Let's call the whole thing off. After all, we're already married.

In the end, the night before waltzing down the damn aisle, we walked Daisy dog down to the river, and talked. Reached across the aisle, and the accents, and opted to rejoice as much in what separated us as what brought us together. Why not be different? As long as I could find a way to be me, and he could find a way to be himself, and we could find space to breathe, as well as a heart to hold, that was all we were after. And that, miraculously, was what we have found. The lesson, in this marriage, as in every other, is to focus on what you love. And on the day? It was all wonderful, and fun and intimate and informal and deeply personal – and very well organised! We both loved it, and each other.

Perhaps the most moving moment of the wedding was my son's short speech. Its raw honesty, by addressing the tumult that had come before the joy, touched a nerve. There wasn't a dry eye in the place. And as I listened with a heart bursting with pride and sadness and joy intermingled, I knew it was one of those rare moments when life hits a sublime harmony.

MY SON'S TOAST

If you had told me, just over four years ago, that I'd be attending this wedding, I would have laughed. If you had told me that I would be standing in front of friends and family, about to deliver something resembling a speech, I would have told you in no uncertain terms to fuck off.

And yet, here I am.

Tim, do you remember the first time we found ourselves alone together? I remember it vividly. It was the last night of my first visit to what had become "your" London and Mom had left on a conveniently unexpected business trip. You promised me something that night, something that turned out to be a complete and utter lie.

We were in the back of a dimly lit neighbourhood pub, driven there by a shared inability to cook. Two men, drinks in hand, trying to avoid silences that alternated between awkward and resentful. In the absence of the person who brought us together, the only glimmer of fellowship that we could muster came in the shape of a common enemy: an unnamed, and at the time unborn, four-legged enemy.

It was there, in that bar, that you promised me you would not accept Mom's latest folly. And yet, on your wedding day, you watched in adoration as our common enemy paraded down the aisle with a pink ribbon in her hair.

Every time that I see Tim stoop down to stare lovingly into Daisy the dog's eyes, I am reminded of his broken promise because, right around the same time, I had made an identical promise to myself: I also would not accept Mom's latest folly.

But just as Tim changed his mind about Mom's new dog, I changed my mind about Mom's new man.

Tim, I am so profoundly grateful that you have entered our lives. Thanks to you I've never had to pick up Daisy's droppings and I no longer think of her as an enemy. Thanks to you and your unequalled empathy, I hear confidence and determination in my sister's voice. Most importantly, thanks to you, I've rediscovered the sound of my mother's laugh. And every time I hear her giggle, I can feel how truly happy she is, new man, new dog, and two old kids in tow.

There is something so damn right about your relationship that I gave up fighting it a long, long time ago. You obviously make each other so deeply happy but you also make those around you feel happier. Your love radiates something so empowering and uplifting that those close to you feel fortunate to be able to bask in it.

It is a real pleasure for me to stand here today and celebrate what you are building. From puppy love, to love with a puppy, to whatever awaits, I look forward to seeing the two of you share a lifetime of bliss.

With all my love.

A FINAL NOTE

Marriage isn't actually "til death do you part," it's actually 'til you're *both* dead that counts. So the wedding is only the first of a series of administrative issues that you will be wise to iron out. From weddings to wills, part of planning your lives together is preparing for a future separation: the death of one of you and its implications until the other one also goes. For us this was another motive to legally wed. Far less romantic than the readings and roses that infused the event itself. Living in the UK, I was stunned to discover how much public policy can influence individual decisions. There is no common law legislation, so couples living together who don't do their homework can be surprised at one or the other's death, that their beloved is not able to keep the house without, above a certain estate level, paying huge (40 percent) inheritance taxes on the current value of the property. And if one of you falls sick, will the other be allowed to make medical decisions for you unless you've expressly appointed them as a beneficiary? Don't be caught short – or let your loved one be.

THREE DRAWERS

I came home from a business trip recently to discover my love had put together my new writing desk. It is a small desk, like its writer. It fits perfectly into the window that has the loveliest view in the house. As soon as I first thought of this window — and this man — as my own, I decided both merited devoted, daily admirers.

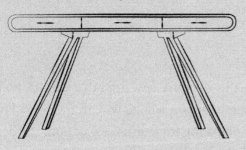

The desk is a slim, dark piece of oak, all rounded into chic, feminine curves. Its non-rectangularness shocks. It occurs to me, seeing it, that it's rare to see curves rather than corners in a desk. It makes you wonder if its writer too may lack — or have grown beyond — her sharper edges. Not that either are demure. The desk boasts three small lacquered drawers in a flashy, unabashed red. "What will you keep in them?" my man asked.

This New Year I resolved to sit daily at this desk. I will write of love. The desk, the window and the man provide a sort of proof-is-in-the-pudding frame. They are also the subject. Gazing from my sunny January window, sitting at the lovingly assembled, red-drawered desk, I know I have made it home. This place, this happiness, was only a theoretical destination of my about-to-turn-50-year-old self. It was a leap out of everything-that-was-approved into nothing-that-was-known. I bet the farm on better. I leapt at a window that might reveal the vision in my heart – and walked out the door. I weep now, in gratitude at my younger self's courage, still cringing at what she had to do.

The new desk invites new directions. Where to go from whole-heartedness? From a destination, it has become a foundation. After so much turbulence, calmer seas are almost unsettling. The achievement of dreams, no matter how often I have now seen it happen, still surprises. 'What next?' It is a question I'd like to flirt with yet a little longer. I want to wander, lost in happiness, just a little further. The next thing will emerge soon enough. It always does. I need to calm my natural impatience to know, to bounce, to plan. And enjoy being right here, right now, with you.

I will learn to sit, and digest the days already consumed like a delicious but not fully appreciated meal. They flew by so fast, these seven extraordinarily intense years. I want to chew through them one more time before they disappear into my ample forgetting. Extract the flavours, smell the roses, bask in the candlelight. Remember the recipe. It seems essential before moving to the next course, which I dream of relishing, whether it is tragically short like my friend Jacquie's, or fashionably long like my mother's or father-in-law's. I will start by writing of love, because for me, the secret of a truly great meal is who you eat it with.

"What will you keep in them?" Everything that matters. In the first, the touch of the man who put them – and me – together. In the next, the curiosity he gifts when he asks what I'm hiding. And, in the last, an ode to this third age we will eat together, day by delicious day.

EPILOGUE: A PARTING WISH

● ● ● ● ● ● ● ● ● ● ● ● ● ● ● ● ● ● ● ●

THIS BOOK IS NOT ONLY A LABOR OF LOVE, it is an ode to love. And vulnerability and truth. It was written as therapy, shared around with compassion, and improved along its journey by the gifts of others' experience. Writing it has allowed me to embrace my story, and listen and learn from many others. My joy has been multiplied by the many people who continue to share their late love stories. I see it reflected in the shining eyes of strangers as they recount their own happy versions. The experience has humbled me often, and lifted me repeatedly. Just yesterday, a 77-year-old neighbour, widowed after 53 years of marriage, came up to me in the street with a mischievous smile. "I have a new late love," she admitted in a hushed, excited whisper, blushing slightly, "Shall I tell you about him?" I nodded in joyful anticipation. The story was beautiful. And life is long. And their story is only just beginning.

Seven years in, that's how I still feel about mine. Blessed, and still becoming. Here is wishing you, too, dear reader, much late love.

CPSIA information can be obtained
at www.ICGtesting.com
Printed in the USA
LVOW04s0204170218
566953LV00001B/1/P